# THERE IS NO
# F*CKING
# SECRET

···········································

# THERE IS
# NO F*CKING
# SECRET

**Letters
from
a Badass
Bitch**

# Kelly Osbourne

G. P. PUTNAM'S SONS   ∗   NEW YORK

PUTNAM

G. P. PUTNAM'S SONS
*Publishers Since 1838*
An imprint of Penguin Random House LLC
375 Hudson Street
New York, New York 10014

Library of Congress Cataloging-in-Publication Data
Names: Osbourne, Kelly, author.
Title: There is no f*cking secret : letters from a badass bitch / Kelly Osbourne.
Other titles: There is no fucking secret
Description: New York : G. P. Putnam's Sons, 2017.
Identifiers: LCCN 2016047463 (print) | LCCN 2017005764 (ebook) | ISBN
9780399176562 | ISBN 9780698409897 (ebook)
Subjects: LCSH: Osbourne, Kelly, date. | Television personalities—
United States—Biography.
Classification: LCC PN1992.4.O73 A3 2017 (print) | LCC PN1992.4.O73 (ebook) |
DDC 791.4502/8092 [B]—dc23
LC record available at https://lccn.loc.gov/2016047463
p.       cm.

Printed in the United States of America
1   3   5   7   9   10   8   6   4   2

*Book design by Lauren Kolm*

*Penguin is committed to publishing works of quality and integrity. In that spirit,
we are proud to offer this book to our readers; however, the story,
the experiences, and the words are the author's alone.*

This book is dedicated to my mumma.

# CONTENTS

# THERE IS NO
# F*CKING
# SECRET

# 1 *

................................................................

# DEAR YOU

Yeah, you! The one reading this book! That's right, I'm talking to you!

I don't know everything, nor do I want to, but in my thirty-odd years of living—and through much trial and error—I have learned a bit. So now I'm going to let you in on a little secret (yeah, yeah, you read the title—there is no "secret," but I'll get to that in a minute): Writing this book has been one of the most intense forms of therapy I have ever experienced. (To find out more on my previous experiences with therapy now, jump to page 181.) It made me realize why I forgot so many things in the first place, no word of a lie.** I could

** TRANSLATION

No word of a lie

The honest truth

write a whole new book about the problems I have now discovered I have through these stumbles, trips, and falling ass-backward down memory lane. However, even when it feels like I'm on the road to

Absolutely Nowhere, I have learned that all I can do is keep putting one foot in front of the other. Sometimes I feel like Dory in *Finding Nemo*, constantly telling myself to "just keep swimming."

As I began what seemed like a monotonous journey of bullet pointing my entire life—from my childhood split between a tour bus and the English countryside to my thoroughly awkward televised teens and twenties (if you're reading this and you're someone I offended in those years, I'm sorry, I was a dick) to my still-fledgling adulthood—I realized just how much I've been through. Some of it was beyond fabulous, and some of it was agonizingly fucked up. Sometimes it made me laugh until I pissed myself, sometimes it made me cry hysterically, and sometimes I'd get so overwhelmed that I'd go into fits of pure rage, which would bring out my inner diva—LizaBeth Taylor (my own personal Sasha Fierce, a combination of Liza Minnelli and Elizabeth Taylor)—and I'd pretend to faint onto the floor of my apartment. Only when I had an audience, of course. If you aren't making someone laugh, you are simply crying alone.

Through all the drama, what has really stood out to me was that no matter what I was writing about, whether it was something really good or really bad, I'd look back at that time and think about how often I felt like complete and utter shit about myself.

If I accomplished something I had worked really hard for, instead of being proud, I'd tell myself I didn't deserve it. Whenever something bad happened, like when my dad would start using again or Mum was diagnosed with cancer, I was convinced that it was 100 percent my fault, even if it was entirely out of my control. I now realize how self-serving this thinking was.

All this made me realize I've always had a hard time big-upping**
myself. So I thought, *Fuck it, I'll do it right now.* That's when I decided to call myself a badass bitch. I've taken more than my fair share
of shit, so I might as well be proud of it.

** TRANSLATION

🇬🇧 Big-upping
🇺🇸 Showing support or
encouragement

My mum grew up working in an industry, and in a time, in which women
were perceived as either bitches or whores.
She taught me that if those were your only
two options, always choose to be the bitch.
To me, a bitch is not a female dog, or a
female asshole—figuratively, not literally—but an outspoken woman
who always takes responsibility for her actions, even when she ruffles a
few feathers along the way.

Let's rewind back to my badass-bitch roots. I grew up in the spotlight, but polish and perfection have never been my strong suits. Take
my family's 1991 appearance on *The Joan Rivers Show.* I was six years
old and proceeded to yawn and scratch my vagina throughout the
entire Father's Day interview. (For more on how this was the somewhat prophetic beginning to a twenty-five-year friendship, turn to
page 41.)

When my family and I innocently decided to let MTV cameras
into our lives for *The Osbournes,* I got thrust into the spotlight, and
let me just tell you that when the glare hit, I did more sweating than
shining. All you had to do was look at my glistening top lip for
evidence.

At that time, we had no idea we were helping to invent reality TV.
Or that people would find us so interesting and weird—or "dysfunctional," as they would say. Although I grew up with famous parents

and infamous grandparents, I was completely unprepared for fame. I just thought it'd be cool to be on MTV. I genuinely did not know that *The Osbournes* would turn me into fair game for the world and the media, who never missed an opportunity to call me fat and twist every personal problem I had into a tabloid headline.

Strangers weren't any better. I'd always been recognized by Ozzy fans, but after the show started, I couldn't walk down the street without being spotted. People were like kids in a candy store—they could not contain their excitement to reveal their opinion of me. Believe me . . . they didn't hold back. Word to the wise: Backhanded compliments, such as "You've got a pretty face for a fat girl" or "You look so much bigger on TV," are *not* real compliments.

When I turned sixteen, I got my driver's license in America, which was a huge deal for me, because in England you couldn't get your license until you were eighteen. The very first time I went for a drive by myself in Los Angeles, I felt like I was on top of the world.

I picked up a friend to take her to one of my favorite cafés. As we were driving there, we noticed a cute guy following us. When he pulled up next to my car, he made that little Grey Poupon signal, à la *Wayne's World*, asking me to roll down the window. I smiled and did, thinking maybe he was going to ask for directions. Instead, he threw a foot-long Subway sandwich in my window, which hit me on the side of my head and exploded. Then he called me a fat bitch and sped off.

My friend was shocked and wanted me to call the police, but I refused. "What do you want me to say?" I asked. "Nine-one-one! I was just assaulted with a Subway foot-long. They'd tell me to fuck off!" I laughed about it, but inside, I was beyond crushed. I would never do something like that to someone who didn't deserve it, and in my eyes, it takes a lot to deserve something like that. After a while, I started to get used to this kind of treatment. In some ways, I even started to think that maybe I'd done something to deserve it.

When my mum got sick with colon cancer and my dad had an ATV accident that put him in a coma and almost killed him, I felt powerless, as if my world were crumbling. During this time, I was under more pressure than ever to keep it together and be there for my family. There is an irony here that, to this day, I struggle to get over and make sense of. It seemed that the more awful things got for us personally, the more famous we became publicly. I constantly wonder, *Do people thrive off the pain and suffering of others?* The sad truth is that some people do.

If you are one of those people, you can stop reading this book now (oh, and you are probably also a sociopath, so perhaps your time is better spent seeking professional help? Just a suggestion) because I am living proof that with the right intentions, hard work, passion, and love for what you do, nothing can stop you.

With my mum in a hospital in Los Angeles and my dad in a hospital in London, my life and career were on hold. Unfortunately, during this time, drugs became my solace and—if I'm being totally honest—probably the only thing that kept me going. With every pill I popped, I retreated more and more into my black hole of self-hatred. By the time I was in my mid-twenties, I'd been through copious amounts of therapy, a few rehabilitation centers, and one mental institution—which worked, because it scared the shit out of me.

I was finally drug-free, but far from a success. I'd replaced drugs with food, and I was broke as a joke. To top it all off, I had to swallow my pride and move back in with my parents. Their house was the only place I was ready to be, because the new drug-free me was still too raw and fragile for the world. Nevertheless, moving back in with my parents after six years of independence made me feel like a failure. Every morning when I woke up to the sweet sounds of my dad stomping around the house like Frankenstein's monster, I would think, *Is this really happening?*

One night during that time, I went to dinner at Mr. Chow's with my dear friend Simon Huck and some of his friends, most of whom I did not know very well at the time. Kim Kardashian (at the time not yet *the* Kim Kardashian) was there. I looked and felt awful and was at one of my lowest points. Kim noticed and asked if she could help. She told me that if I ever needed anything, I could call her. She could introduce me to trainers or take me to the gym. In Hollywood, unless the cameras are on or the checkbook is out, you won't find many people willing to step up and help you, and I will always be grateful to Kim for the fact that she did. But as soon as the words were out of her mouth, I knew I would never take her up on her offer because I was too embarrassed to put on gym clothes and stand next to someone with a body like hers, when I had a little dumpling body like mine.

Her genuine concern stuck out to me, because I knew she really meant it. It was also a wake-up call. If someone I barely knew at the time took one look at me and knew something was wrong, then I must have been fucking miserable.

It was time for me to get my shit together, so I did.

I decided to go on *Dancing with the Stars*. Being on that show turned me into an adult. It was a true journey of self-discovery. It taught me that yes, I'm Sharon and Ozzy Osbourne's daughter, but

I'm not just someone's kid. I'm me. I'm enough with them and I'm enough without them.

I wish I could say it's been all up from there, but there have been a few bumps. I was a fucked-up ugly duckling who somehow emerged a lavender swan. I went from being the girl mums told their kids to stay away from to the girl mums follow on social media and stop in the street to ask for advice about their own daughters' struggles. I went from being taunted as a worthless celebrity spawn to being a woman with her own career who the media respects, albeit sometimes begrudgingly.

I managed to defy everyone's expectations, but most important, I also managed to defy my own. The reaction to this, of course, was a gigantic, collective "What the fuck?" Everyone wanted to know what I had done and how I'd done it. Interviewers, celebrities struggling with demons of their own, bloggers, and even the barista where I went to get my morning tea wanted to know "What's your secret?!"

The way everyone asked, it was as if they expected me to clue them in to some magical milk shake I drink every night before bed, or a cave I crawled into for a month and emerged skinny and slick with confidence, with "Eye of the Tiger" playing in the background. The first few times, I laughed it off, then I started to think, *This is mental!* Did they not see how long this actually took? It was not instant—it took years! I guess people pick up on your journey only when you arrive at your destination.

So after fielding the same question what seemed about fifty million times, I decided to write this book, because: THERE IS NO FUCKING SECRET!

If there were one, and I had it, I would have told the world the first chance I got—I'm not the kind of person who tries to hoard the good stuff for myself. Instead, all I can do is share what worked for me, and the dedication it took to get where I am today. It's still a work in progress. Isn't everything?

I truly believe that the first step to transformation is pulling your head out of your ass and deciding to transform! Much to my dismay, no one came along and did it for me, and the same goes for you. Sure, this can be daunting, but it's also incredibly empowering—it means you don't have to wait for someone to give you permission, because your life is finally in your hands.

To make any kind of positive change, you have to accept yourself for who you are right now, not some imagined dream girl (or guy) who has zero wobbly bits and never needs to fart. You have to realize that this airbrushed perfection we've been sold all our lives is unattainable. It's not even something to work toward—it's just a straight-up lie. You will never be perfect, I will never be perfect, no one will ever be perfect, because *perfection does not exist.*

After you've got that in your head, the next step is learning to love your imperfect self, which, let's face it, is easier said than done. In spite of how you may feel about yourself, I truly believe that each of us is unique, individual, and beautiful—it's simply whether you can find the bravery within yourself to show it to the world.

It's taken me a few decades and more than a few mishaps to get to this point. With all that said, I now sincerely know that I don't want to be the prettiest girl in the room, or the smartest—I don't even want to be the best. I just want to be me.

Through my years of therapy, writing has always helped me put all my crazy, mixed-up thoughts into an order I can understand. There have been times in my life when the only way I could communicate with my loved ones was through writing letters—some that I wrote with no intention of ever sending (I pray that no one ever reads the drafts folder in my e-mail.) Doing so helped me find my voice and express myself in the way I really wanted to be heard. With this book, I decided to write letters to all the people, places, situations, accusations, and liberations that have transpired to make me *me*.

I want you to laugh along with me at my crazy life. My hope is that when you finish this book, you will be inspired to write a few letters of your own. I implore you to embrace all the weird and wonderful things that make you *you*, and so unique to this world. Trust me, you'll be surprised what you discover about yourself and shocked at how brave you really are.

 *Love,*
*Kelly O*

# 2 *

......................................................................

# DEAR INNER FILTER
## (OR LACK THEREOF)

Where have you been all my life? No, seriously, where the fuck have you been? Because I can't remember you ever existing. As far back as I can recall, it's just been me and my mouth, getting in trouble everywhere we go.

First off, can you believe that I wasn't even allowed to curse until I moved to America? It's hard to fathom, right? Considering that I am an Osbourne and it seems like we should have come out of the birth canal with a mouth like a sailor. But no, those filthy fucking mouths were made, not born. This does not mean we are any less proud of them.

With that said, I want to take this time to issue a clear warning: If you have a problem with profanity and are offended easily, you should probably go read a different book. The Bible, perhaps? Oh no, wait—there's plenty of debauchery in that one. Some Shakespeare, then. No, wait, not that, either . . . Oh, fuck it . . . if you don't like profanity and are easily offended, then just get on with it and go read *Chicken Soup for the Fucking Soul* or some shit like that, okay?

The same goes with talking about vaginas or bodily functions—if you are offended by the mention of those, then this is also not the book for you. (If you are not offended by vaginas, then you might want to turn to page 117, where I wrote a letter to mine.)

I honestly don't know how I ended up with a career that finds me frequently on live television or in front of a live audience, because I don't know that this mouth is made for it. I'm like somebody who has been injected with truth serum and is incapable of keeping her thoughts to herself. It all comes out.

When I was in the second grade, my family moved to America for just one year. For some insane reason, Mum sent us kids to an extremely conservative Christian school, where we were labeled troublemakers from the first day we set foot in the building. I guess it makes sense, though: When your dad is the Prince of Darkness, you're a walking billboard for sin.

Once the teachers even took it upon themselves to lock my sister and me in a pitch-black bathroom, where we were instructed to pray because "Daddy was a Satanist." At first, we cried; then we started to giggle. I suddenly realized, *Well, they have to let us out when Mum comes to pick us up, and if we have to wee, the toilet's right there.* I decided we actually had it pretty good, as being locked in a dark, pissy bathroom still seemed better than sitting in class.

One of the first times I can remember bearing the brunt of my inability to discern what was okay to say and what wasn't was at that school. I got suspended and had to sit in the dreaded red chair outside the headmaster's office because I told some kids in my class what sex was. I was eight, so my description was far from graphic and more along the lines of "When a daddy really loves a mummy, he puts his penis in . . . ," but the school had a fit on behalf of Adam and Eve. It ain't my fault they ate the fucking apple. My attempts to enlighten my fellow second-graders to the glorious and godly act of procreation were definitely not smiled upon.

Sometimes my indiscretions were just the result of words meaning something different in the UK from what they mean in the US. (For example, did you know *trump* means "fart" in England? Asking "Who trumped?" is the equivalent of asking "Who tooted?") When I asked a kid at school if I could borrow his rubber, I got sent to the principal's office for being naughty. I had no idea what I had done. I wasn't rude—I'd asked very politely! All I'd wanted was to use his eraser . . .

As an adult, my inner filter remains porous, and I still find myself in constant trouble. On the few occasions when I am able to keep my mouth shut, it's my face that decides to tell it like it is. I recently was looking at photos of Mum and me from a photo shoot for a charity event for a wonderful organization that does amazing things run by incredible people, so my feelings about the photos had nothing to do with them. But someone had the bright idea that Mum and I would wear white gowns and smash chocolate cake all over each other.

The result? We looked like tampons covered in shit. Mum was hysterical, while I was half blind from getting frosting in my eye. My resting bitch face was visible from the studio in Los Angeles all the way to England.

I work in a deranged industry. I love it, clearly, but Hollywood is insane, and occasionally I'll find myself in a situation that makes me feel like I'm the only one who hasn't drunk the Kool-Aid. For example, I can be at a shoot where everyone is spending twenty-five minutes looking at two photographs that are exactly the same, taken a split second apart, and trying to decide which one to use. "Do you like this one," someone will ask me, "or this one?" Meanwhile, the clock is ticking, and I can't tell them apart to save my life. In these kinds of moments, someone like my makeup artist Denika will come up and whisper in my ear, "Look a little happier."

Boom! That snaps me back to reality, because I don't ever want to appear ungrateful or unhappy. It's just that faking it until I make it has never been part of my repertoire.

Many celebrities have a contrived image that they strive to keep up in public, but my mum always taught us that the fewer skeletons we have in our closet, the less people have to dig up. With me, what you get is what you see, and when you don't have a lot of secrets, it's easy to speak your truth. I'm done trying to be anyone else, and if that gets me in trouble sometimes, I'm okay with that. It means I'm honest.

Unfortunately, honesty can sometimes be misconstrued as being mean. If I ever feel like I've been mean, personally offensive, or unintentionally hurtful to someone, then I will be the first to call and apologize (if I meant to hurt your feelings, you will know it, and anyways, fuck you). There can be such a thing as too much honesty, and a huge part of having good manners is being able to read a situation and know when the truth will do more harm than good—especially when it's none of your business.

I will never say I'm sorry for refusing to play the game that sanitizes our emotions and who we are as people. Women especially are archaically taught early on to say the right things, never make a fuss, and certainly never do anything that would make anyone else uncomfortable. We learn to subvert our own feelings just so we won't make anyone else feel bad. If we don't put our own needs absolutely last, then we know what's coming: the dreaded B-word. BITCH. Someone's always got something to say about everything I do. I mean, they can turn a fart into something controversial, while I'm thinking, *Come on. Get over it. Everyone farts.*

There's not one thing in this world that I can do that somebody isn't going to tell me I'm a fool for, and I say, Fuck that. I'm glad you, inner filter, are broken. If being honest, standing up for myself, and staying true to who I am makes me a bitch, then fine, I'll be a bitch. I'm the biggest bitch on earth, and that's a label I'll wear proudly.

*Love,*
*Kelly O*

# 3 *

· · · · · · · · · · · · · · · · · · · · · · · · · · · · · · · · · · · · · · · · · · · · · · · · · · · · · · · · · · · · · · · · · · · · · · · · · · · · · ·

# DEAR FITTING IN

Are you aware of just how boring and overrated you are?

However, to be entirely fair, I'm not exactly speaking from experience here, as I've never really known what you feel like. I honestly can't remember a single time or place in my life where I ever felt as though I truly 100 percent fit in.

Growing up, I was led to believe my family was just like everybody else's, which, of course, could not be further from the truth. God bless my mother, though. She did everything she could to protect my siblings and me. And for a long time, it really did work. But the fact is, my world was either the countryside in England, climbing trees with my brother and sitting on my "thinking swing" under my favorite tree, or tour buses and backstage passes. Our friends were everyone from the band members of my father's opening acts to roadies to vendors to truck drivers to record company executives. If we were lucky, one of the opening-band members might also have kids who came for the show. For example, when Geezer Butler was playing bass, his kids, Biff and James, would always come on tour. When Sepultura was with us, our numbers grew, because Max Cavalera has five kids! It was awesome.

I especially loved the summertime, when I was allowed to bring my two best friends, Sammy and Fleur. We were all perceived as outcasts, but everyone came together as one big extended family. It didn't matter that our dad was the star of the show; Mum never let us think we were better than anyone else, and no one ever treated us as if we were. Unlike a typical household, where kids are lucky enough to have one or even two parental figures to call them out on their shit, we were surrounded by dozens of grown-ups, who were ready, willing, and able to call us out on ours. There was no "get out of jail free" card for me. This was the real game of Life, not Monopoly.

*Normal* wasn't even a word in my vocabulary, so in this environment, I didn't know that I was "different." The first school I went to was the Gateway School in the village of Great Missenden. Everything about it was idyllic. It was pulled from a children's book, as it had been the setting for most of Roald Dahl's greatest novels. His children and grandchildren also went to school there. Gateway was the kind of school that any parent would give their left arm for their children to attend, which explained why every morning and afternoon, my mum would change clothes and put on a floral Laura Ashley dress to drop us off and pick us up.

Maybe the other mothers wondered why Sharon Osbourne seemed to own only three dresses, but beyond that, they couldn't judge, because those dresses were just like theirs. Eventually, she gave up and just wore her robe. That was just one of the little ways we tried to blend in over the years, but to no avail—eventually Dad got banned from parent-teacher conferences for being intoxicated, farting, falling asleep, and lifting up his shirt to see if he'd lost any weight in the short ten minutes he was sitting there.

Here's the thing about being a celebrity's kid: In some ways, it's amazing, and many kids of celebs are very fortunate, especially if their parents have been financially successful enough to mean that they're well-off. There can also be a downside, especially when you're too young to recognize how fortunate you are and the only thing that you really do know is that you're different from everybody else.

I remember being in geography class and the teacher asking if anyone had been to Milan. I had, so I raised my hand. She refused to call on me. Instead, she announced to the entire class, "Anyone besides you, Miss Osbourne. We all know your daddy's rich and famous and you've traveled the world." If the other kids hadn't already realized I was different, they certainly did after that.

My parents always encouraged me to embrace my differences. Due to their own extremely public life choices and who they are, they can't be hypocrites. Even when they didn't approve of the ways I decided to artistically express myself, they gave me the gift of freedom of self-expression. (For some reason, this practice has not carried over into adulthood. Not a day goes by in which my mother doesn't not-so-subtly hint that she hates my shaved head because it makes me look "hard" or my father offers to give me exorbitant amounts of money if only I would "grow my goldilocks back," since as a child my hair really was the color of gold.) At thirteen, when everyone I knew was wearing

JNCO jeans and wallet chains, I did everything I could, and any extra chores possible, to convince my mum to buy me a pair of brown-and-white Prada men's golf shoes and a bright yellow Dolce & Gabbana jacket with a leopard-print lining. (Dolce & Gabbana + Prada = a fuckload of chores.) I remember wearing these together, with my hair in Princess Leia buns, blue cat-eye glasses, and braces, further accessorized with a skateboard that I carried because I thought it made me look cool but did not know how to ride.

The shoes had metal spikes on the bottom, so as I clopped down the 3rd Street Promenade in Santa Monica, you could hear me coming from miles away. I was worse than a legion of horses. I thought I was unstoppably cool, even though when I looked around, no one looked like me. I did not care—I felt amazing and I looked like myself. In my opinion, that is way better than fitting in.

Overnight, the MTV show turned me from simply someone's kid—still notorious in certain circles, but primarily anonymous—into one of the most famous teenagers in the world. It wasn't as if it were something I'd worked long and hard for and could gradually enjoy. One day, we were just us, the Osbournes. The day after the series premiere, we were The Osbournes. Paparazzi had never given a fuck about me before, but now they were waiting wherever I went. Even with no cameras in sight, I was still the freak show. I'd see people sneaking their phones out and whispering, or I could hear them walking faster and faster behind me to try to catch up.

I always try my hardest not to be rude, because if it weren't for the people in this world, many of whom support my career, I wouldn't have the life I have. However, I would be lying if I didn't admit to the times that I snapped at the rudeness that I often encountered. When

I did, it was usually in response to comments aimed at my family. When that happened, I could (and still do to this day) occasionally lose my shit. It's not just my family I defend. I am a firm believer in standing up for yourself, and I hold myself to that standard as well. Like the time I got into a screaming match with a total stranger in the Meatpacking District in New York City.

I was leaving the Boom Boom Room with friends, and as we were trying to get in a cab to go home, amid what seemed like a crowd of hundreds on every corner vying to get into some new hotspot, all anyone could hear over the cacophony of an extremely raucous crowd was the voice of a pitiful stranger in a Tweety Bird shirt yelling, "Fuck you, Kelly Osbourne, you cunt, you're fat and ugly." Needless to say, I handed that puddy tat her ass.

When I look back, I realize how much of my teenage years were spent trying to convince people I wasn't who they thought I was, when all the while I really should have just been telling them to piss off.**

** TRANSLATION

🇬🇧 Piss off
🇺🇸 Mind your own business

Even among the other celebrity spawn, I still didn't fit in because I don't look like a supermodel. As I got older, I'd overcompensate for this and do things to prove that I was at least worthy of the attention I was getting. (Dad told me once that he used to do the same thing when he was young.) If someone dared me, I had no qualms about accepting, especially if I had a drink in me. This is how I came to hold the record for doing the most shots in one night at Bungalow 8.

The signature shot there was a super-fruity concoction that barely even tasted like it had alcohol in it. I ordered so many that they ceased to give them to me in shot glasses and instead handed me a glass jug and a stack of cups when I walked in. On the night in question, I was with cute boys who I wanted to impress, and I did twenty-five shots and drank all those guys under the table.

I didn't get hangovers in those days, so the next morning, I was up and right back to work. When you think about it, hangover or no, it's pretty sad, really, the lengths I thought I had to go to just to be around people who were really idiots.

Wherever I went, people knew my parents' reputation, so there was a preconceived notion of who I was going to be before I even walked in the door. People either expected me to be like my mum, a no-nonsense boss bitch who could take control of any situation, or they expected me to be a total hell-raiser like my dad. The truth is, I am a combination of the two—a recipe that makes me unique, unpredictable, and fun. As it turns out, when people judge you before knowing you, you have an advantage. Instead of being angry and defensive, I have learned to turn the judgments into something positive—an opportunity to wake up every day and pleasantly surprise all the ignorant dumbasses just by being myself.

**✱✱ TRANSLATION**

🇬🇧 Dead normal
🇺🇸 Extremely normal

For example, a couple of years ago, I went to Liverpool to visit my friend Jay, stay with his family, and hang out with his friends. After I left, everyone told Jay how shocked they were.

"She's dead normal,"✱✱ they said, amazed that I hadn't been a complete cunt.

Jay, to his credit, was equally shocked that they would have expected otherwise. "What, do you think I'd hang out with an asshole?" he shot back.

Ha. Eat my shit!

People love to say that they have no regrets because they have learned from their mistakes. I, too, have learned from my mistakes, and I continue to do so. I do have one regret: I regret all the time I wasted trying to be anyone but myself. It's fucking hard trying to be someone else, not to mention miserable. I spent so much of my life and energy dreaming about how all my problems would be solved if I just looked a certain way, or acted a certain way, or just had someone else's completely different life. Too bad there, because the life we've got is the only one we'll ever get, which is exactly why we've got to accept it and make it count.

This thinking can be exhausting and sad. Wanting to fit in or be somebody else can manifest in all sorts of negative ways. I remember once meeting a girl at an event and looking down at her feet, which were squeezed into a pair of Louboutins that were at least a size and a half too small for her. It was like Cinderella's ugly stepsister trying to make the shoe fit. This girl wore them all day long, even though her skin was shredding off where the shoes rubbed against her feet. Clearly, they hurt like hell.

Here you see a desperation and a need to fit in that are so strong that someone is willing to put herself through actual physical pain in an attempt to present the image that she's someone who wears a certain type of shoe. What's the point in that? It's a shoe. You can get a different shoe that fits, or wait until your size comes in! Because let me tell you, sweetness, those flesh-toned Louboutins are the company's biggest seller. They ain't going anywhere, no matter how badly you think you need them right now.

The girl's shoes stood out to me because I recognized a bit of myself in her, in how much I'd put myself through trying to pass myself off as anything but who I really was. I've finally learned that I can only be me, and even though I'm fucking nuts, it is in the best way possible.

My struggles with my weight and with drugs all stemmed from the fact that I didn't like who I was. I never thought I was skinny enough or good enough or smart enough. What I finally realized was that there's no reward for being a sheep. No matter who you date, what clothes you wear, or what car you drive, if you base your life off other people and what they have, you will always feel inferior. You will never have enough, and you will not be happy. For me, I finally hit a wall where I just didn't want to be miserable anymore. I wanted to stop wishing I was a certain size or a certain pedigree, or pretending to be a person I wasn't so that someone I barely even knew wouldn't think poorly of me.

What I know now is that just because there isn't anyone like you doesn't mean you're alone. I honestly feel like I identify with drag queens more than I do with anyone else, because they are unidentifiable. They choose how the world sees them, and they usually do this even when they know they're going to have to take a shitload of abuse for it. I think that is magical.

Society tells you that you have to fit in and encourages you to find people who are just like yourself, but if you only know people who are just like yourself, then you are nothing but a lemming.

Only being around people like you may be comfortable for a while, but it's also boring. If you were to look through my Rolodex, you would see everyone from members of the Royal Family to convicted felons currently serving time. None of them are "just like me." No one is, but I don't think that's so bad anymore. Instead, I know how lucky

I am to know people who have totally different experiences and ways of looking at the world. We get along and accept one another's flaws. And when you think about it, if you can get along, then who gives a fuck if you fit in?

*Love,*
*Kelly O*

# 4 *

......................................................................................................

# DEAR MUM

You are the baddest bitch I know. I love you more than anything.

I could leave it at that, because with a woman like you, *the* Sharon Osbourne, where do I even start? You're beautiful, so smart, an amazing mother and businesswoman, you're funny and fun and ridiculous and fabulous, and you're my mum. I'm so fucking lucky.

Throughout your entire life, you have had no choice but to be tough, but I am continually astonished by just how tough you are.

You have taught me everything I know, from how to brush my teeth to what it means to work hard to how to be glamorous and gracious at the same time. You live by the philosophy that you give everyone your full respect—until they do something to prove they don't deserve it. You always taught me that I'll see the same people on the way up as I will on the way down and, oh, they'll remember. You treat everyone equally, whether they're the CEO of a major company or someone selling T-shirts at a merch stand. You made a lot of sacrifices so that our family could have the life we had, but at the same time, you always reminded me that I could never, ever think I'm better than anyone. I'm never too good to wait in a line, make myself a sandwich, or clean my own fucking toilet.

You and I are alike in that we love to be silly and don't give a fuck what other people think about it. You don't give a second thought to doing a stupid impression or dancing a jig across the dining room of a really posh restaurant. I love that about you. Going back to the days when you used to flash your tits at the school bus, you never fail to make me laugh, even if I'm wishing I could melt into the floor at the same time.

You and I will still have the little mother-daughter differences of opinion that have always been, and always will be, there for everyone. As I write this, I'm wearing my Adidas slide sandals. If I'm not at an event wearing heels, these are almost always on my feet, and I know you hate them. You call them my "prison flip-flops," after all! "Kelly," you'll say, your voice dropping as if what you are about to say is really embarrassing, "they wear them on *Orange Is the New Black!*"

Finally, you had had enough and went out and bought me some new slides—from fucking Givenchy! I call these my "French prison flip-flops." Then you followed up with a pair of Célines, which I call my "Japanese prison flip-flops," because they look like ninja shoes and also make a farting noise with every step I take. These are very sweet gestures—but it did make me feel like a fucking twat walking around in a pair of high-fashion fancy flip-flops! They also cut the shit out of my feet, so the only way I can wear them is with a big, thick pair of fuzzy athletic socks. That really offends people, but for me, it makes them just about right. You had to know I would do something to make them mine.

You are one of the hardest-working people I have ever met in my entire life. Even when you were in the hospital having chemotherapy, I would have to snatch the phone out of your hands because nothing could stop you.

You told me about all the business plans and how you ran the company, what your wishes were and what you worried about. Now it makes me shudder, because I know that you were telling me all this so I would know what to do if you did not make it, but as a result I really got to know you. Not just as Mum but as an individual human being. A person.

I never thought I would be lucky enough to understand you the way that I do now. Thank you for never giving up on me, even when I was blaming you for everything that was going wrong. I spent a lot of time in my teens and early twenties trying to do whatever I could to make myself different. Like all teenage girls, I had this ridiculous fear of turning into you, Mum.

When I finally allowed myself to do some growing up, I woke up one morning and realized that I *am* you! How could I not be? I had been fighting the inevitable for so long, and now I embrace it! I am so proud to be your daughter.

Mum, you are the most beautiful, generous, kind, and loving person I could ever know. You came from a generation when not many women worked outside the home, and I know that this has always made you terrified that people would think you were a bad mother. This couldn't be further from the truth—you were, and still are, the best mum! You gave us an amazing childhood that I wouldn't trade for anything else in the world.

The public perception of me is that I am a daddy's girl, but Mum, I will always be your soldier. I will always have your back, because you threw yourself in front of a bus for my siblings and me. Most people think that saving Dad and his career was your number one priority, when really it was providing a better life for us than the one that you had. You have achieved that goal tenfold. If I inherited even 1 percent of your strength, talent, and beauty, I'm not only lucky but set for life. What more can I say? I love you.

*Love,*
*Kelly O*

# 5 *

. . . . . . . . . . . . . . . . . . . . . . . . . . . . . . . . . . . . . . . . . . . . . . . . . . . . . . . . . . . . .

# DEAR DAD

Out of all the letters I've written, this is the hardest, because you are my father but also my best friend. Yeah, you're not perfect, and you fuck up a lot—A LOT—and you're still pretending to be deaf when I know you can hear me, but I fucking love you and will always be Daddy's little girl.

My childhood may have been very different and backward, but I consider myself lucky. Some people have real piece-of-shit parents, but I don't. Sure, you both have flaws, but I've never doubted how much you love me. It's amazing how much you can get through with love.

Norman Rockwell is one of my favorite artists, and when we were growing up, Mum had a coffee table book of his paintings and owned several of his pieces (which are now hanging on Jack's wall, much to my annoyance). I used to sit there and stare at the book, slowly turning the pages and taking in every image—happy people gathered around a turkey dinner or fathers reading to their children. The one thing I knew about Rockwell was that he painted "perfect" families. *Wow,* I would think, *if that's what a family is supposed to look like, we're nothing like that.*

Through all the years that you were an active addict, Dad, almost any family outing, event, or celebration ended in shit, even though I sometimes didn't even realize it was bad. At one of my birthday parties, you rounded us all up in the garden shed to play Three Little Pigs. When it came time to shout "I'll huff and I'll puff and I'll blow your house down," you popped out the door wearing the werewolf mask from your *Bark at the Moon* music video and album cover. Every kid started screaming and crying their eyes out. They were all so inconsolable they got sent home, while I was sitting there thinking it was hilarious and wondering what had happened to my party.

For many years, Dad, you made my life a living hell. Even as a child, I never questioned your addiction or the god complexes that came along with your career as a rock star. I just saw what was in front of me and figured I had to find a way to love you as you were, because you were the only father I was ever going to get.

You and Mum never lied to us about your addictions. You always told us what drugs were and what you were going through. The way you explained it was that your heart and soul were saying no, but your body and brain were saying yes. The body and brain were telling you that without drugs, you would die, so they almost always won.

When there is an active addict in the family, everyone chooses to deal with it differently. Some people choose to face things head-on, which is fucking hard, if not impossible; others decide to just never be around or create their own delusions. I chose to create my own delusions, because, Dad, you were my hero.

Aimee was always with Mum, and Jack was running around with his friends, so often it was just me and you. I don't know if the role was given to me, or if I took it on myself, but I became the one in our family who took care of everybody else. When it came to you, my default was to clean up your messes. Sometimes, that was literal, as I'd be on my hands and knees with a rag, wiping up puke before anyone else saw it. Other times, it was more spiritual, as I'd tried to gloss things over by saying, "Oh, that never happened," or would figure out a way to distract everyone so they'd shine the light on me and spend less time looking in the shadows.

Dad, you are a rare breed of human being who, no matter what you do, will somehow always manage to get away with it. There's something so fucking innocent about you, even though your behavior is devilish. You have a special kind of charm that also takes a lot of bravery and a massive ego, and you are one of the best liars in the world.

The only people you have never lied to are your fans, and they are the only ones who bring out your humble side. I'll never forget a show at Voodoo Fest in New Orleans, when it was pouring rain. The field was still packed, even though the fans were soaked to the skin and getting wetter by the minute. The stage was protected, so you could have easily performed the entire set and only gotten hit with a few droplets. Instead, you walked onstage with your hands in a yogi prayer position, bowing to the crowd over and over again before taking a couple of buckets of water and pouring them over your head to show the audience that you were right there with them. You may have bitten off the head of a bat, Dad, but you would never, ever bite the hand that feeds you.

No matter what mistakes you have made in your personal life and in your role as my father, there is no way I could have anything but respect for the fact that you are almost seventy years old at the time of this writing and still selling out seventy-thousand-plus-seat arenas and running around the stage for two and a half hours a night. I would challenge anyone to find a nineteen-year-old who puts on a better show than you, Dad.

The media has crafted an image of you where you're a bumbling, deaf fool who never knows what's going on, but this couldn't be further from the truth. Playing dumb is part of your act. I know this, so I would never fuck with you because people have no idea how smart you are.

You remember absolutely everything when it comes to me. More than once you have repeated to me something that I said, verbatim, six months before, when you were in a different room and I didn't even know you were listening. Hard of hearing, my ass.

Dad, if someone is lucky enough to have you love them—and there are very few people you love, outside of our family—you will love them forever. You are very old-school, in that when a woman walks into the room, whether she's nineteen or ninety, you stand up to give her your seat, and you have always seen yourself as the provider in the family.

Dad, when you are sober, I cannot find a better person on earth, or someone with a bigger heart. It makes me very happy that my nieces could possibly go their whole lives without ever knowing you as a using addict, and they will remember you only as the loving, caring person you truly are. They adore you, especially Pearl, and the feeling is mutual.

For a long time, I always thought I was more like my mother, but, ironically, it's only been recently that I have started to see how much I am truly you—but with a vagina and minus the sex addiction. I got your sense of mischievousness, where I will always want to push buttons just to see how far I can go, and I even look like you. I have the same eyes, same jaw, and even your legs! I can read you better than anyone else in the family, and know what you want before you even ask for it.

We each have the same morning routine, where we'll get up, put on our workout clothes, then waffle around for an hour while we put off actually going to the gym. We were once traveling together and I put on some music. "Are you listening to *Abbey Road*?" you asked. I said yes, and that I listened to the whole album every day.

"So do I," you said.

It had been so long since we'd lived together, I had no idea.

I'm the only one in the family who goes to hang out with you, just to sit and watch crap TV and talk about nothing. You never cease to surprise me with what you know, asking me if something you read in a gossip mag is actually true. I'm just sitting there thinking, *When the fuck did you get a copy of* Us Weekly? *And then take the time to read it?* Or I'll walk into the kitchen and find you singing Demi Lovato's "Cool for the Summer."

"Dad, do you even know who sings this song?" I'll ask.

"No, but I like it. It's shitty pop music."

"Shitty pop music" is how you classify everything you think someone with the nickname "The Prince of Darkness" shouldn't like. It always cracks me up. You're the same way with my dog, Polly—you don't want to like her, because she's cute and you think you should only like things that are scary, but I've seen you cuddle her and I know you love her!

As much as you have put me through, Dad, I know you will always protect me. You hate when I wear anything low-cut, and you have your assistants stalk me on social media. If there's something you don't like on my Instagram, you don't even know what it is and will tell me what you saw "on your Internet." "I don't have an Internet, Dad," I'll tell you. "It's *the* Internet." We've had this same conversation dozens of times.

Your bandmates are my extended family, and I have watched them grow up just as they have watched me. Over the decades, I've seen the backstage turn from a circus of groupies and substances to cheese plates and fruit trays and whispers because Geezer's taking a pre-show nap. I've never loved the holidays—probably because no one knows how to ruin a good time like you, Dad—but when I'm backstage at Black Sabbath or one of your shows, I imagine I feel like normal people do on Christmas morning. Surrounded by a multigenerational, tight-knit group of people I love, some of whom have known me since the day I was born. It might not be Norman Rockwell, but it's as close as I'm going to get. I wouldn't trade it for anything. I love you, Dad.

*Love,*
*Kelly O*

# 6 *

........................................................................................

# DEAR JACK

The day you were born, I got a best friend for life. The days your daughters, Pearl and Andy Rose, were born, I discovered a new kind of love and happiness that I didn't even know existed. I admire you more than any man I've ever met, and I will always be proud to be your big sister.

For most of the big things that have happened in our family, you have always been the one to break the news to me. All you need to do is say my name, and I can tell from the tone of your voice that it is going to be something serious. That is why, when you called me about four years ago and said, "Kelly, we need to talk, can I come over?" I fucking shit myself. What was it this time? Something with Mum? With Dad?

I had this giant yellow pleather bed that had three matching yellow pleather steps that I could pull up to the side, so that the dogs could get in bed with me. When you got there, you walked right in and sat on the bed. I just kept thinking, *Oh my God, oh my God, this must be serious*, but then you said, "Kelly, I'm going to have a baby. Lisa's pregnant."

Immediately, I started screaming and felt like I was going to cry—from pure happiness. As exciting as that moment was, it was also good-bye in a way, because—and I don't know if you noticed this—that was the last time I got to be a big sister to you, my little brother.

Growing up, you and I were practically twins. While Aimee got her own room on tour, you and I shared one. We made the same friends, had the same clothes—elastic-waist jeans from Marks & Spencer—and got in trouble for the same shit. Whenever anything happened in the house, Mum just punished both of us, as that was easier than trying to figure out who had actually done it.

As we got older, it got harder for us to get along, and we weren't always partners in crime. You matured a lot earlier than I did. You were given the role of the man of the house at such a young age. You also got sober at seventeen, after just one trip to rehab, but had to watch me flounder through my late teens and early twenties. I know that you were pissed at me for not getting my shit together but also sad about what I was doing to myself. I don't blame you.

When I finally started to grow up, we were as close as ever again, and we have remained so. It might sound weird, but as happy as I was when Lisa joined the family, it was hard for me to adjust to not being the first person you call with news anymore. Still, it has made me very proud to watch you grow up and see the man you have become. Now I am learning more about life from my little brother than I have from anybody else, ever. You learned to set boundaries a lot earlier than I did, and you took the steps you needed to remove yourself from the drama that always engulfs our family.

Jack, you have always been hardworking and brave, and I know you truly want to make the world a better place. It makes me so happy to see that you now have a wife and two little girls who are the beneficiaries of your benevolence. I can see in your eyes how much you love your babies and how much they absolutely adore you back. It's really a beautiful thing to watch. You are by no means perfect, but you're a really good dad and a generally good person. (Thanks for making me look bad, asshole.)

Having a child is a lot of work, and your life had to change a lot for it. Some people aren't willing to make those changes, but you and Lisa have gone above and beyond from the moment you realized you were going to be parents. The first time I watched you argue about who was going to change a diaper, I thought, *Oh my god, you're not a baby anymore!*

Pearl and Andy Rose have been the best things to ever happen to our family, and you gain a whole new respect for life when you watch a new family member grow up. Last Christmas, when you and Lisa were busy in the kitchen making dinner, Pearl asked me what a certain . . . let's just call it *colorful* word meant. I basically shit myself and I don't think anyone has seen me change a subject so quickly. You and Lisa are always so good at handling those kinds of situations. I wasn't going to be the one to answer difficult questions, especially without you there to help me out! Without missing a beat I started singing, "Let it go, let it go . . . ," and she instantly started singing along with me. Thank you, *Frozen*, for helping Pearl and me to let go of that chillingly awkward situation.

Jack, when you were diagnosed with MS, one of my first thoughts was, *Why him? I've done way more bad shit and been more of an asshole than he ever has. He doesn't deserve this!* You are through and through a soldier, and I know that the last thing you would ever want is for someone to treat you as though you're sick. You'll never admit when you're having a flare, but because I know you so well, I can tell by the way you walk or the squint to your eyes. I've learned to make jokes about it and call you Captain Jack Sparrow when I notice it. I'll tap you on the shoulder and say, "Aye aye, Captain," and it's our little signal that I know what's going on and that if you need anything, I'm there.

Jack, you and I always thought of ourselves as two halves of the same person because we did everything together. We now recognize that we can have our own lives, be different, and still be close. You have a male perspective and I have a female perspective, so sometimes we don't see eye to eye on things. There are some things we just don't talk about, and while I don't always understand the way you think, I will always respect it, because you've seen a lot and are very wise. I also want to thank you, Lisa, for always defending me when I am right and helping me to see my brother's perspective when I am wrong.

No matter what happens in our family, or how much we each grow and change as people, I love you unconditionally. It's an honor to be your big sister—but still, if you flick my ear one more time, I will kick your fucking ass.

*Love,*
*Kelly O*

# 7 *

························································

# DEAR JOAN

There is not a day that goes by that I don't think of you and laugh, and cry a bit, because I miss you so much. Yes, yes, I know, you'd prefer I'd quit it with the crying bullshit and just stick to the laughter, but you bitch, I just can't help it, okay? After twenty-five years of friendship, I am constantly remembering the good times.

For example, once when I was on a flight to New York, I was dead tired and fell asleep before the plane had even left the ground. When I woke up upon arrival, I couldn't see anything and momentarily thought I'd gone blind, or maybe that I was even dead.

Then I realized it was a piece of paper. Taped to my forehead. I ripped it off, thinking, *What kind of maniac tapes a piece of paper to another passenger's forehead?!* Then I realized it was a note:

"Kell!!! You must stop stalking me! xoxox Look in 3H! You have a friend! ☺ Joan PS-Do you need a lift? PS2-You don't snore."

I turned around, and sure enough, there you were, giving me a little wave from 3H, quite pleased with yourself for having talked the flight attendants into giving you some tape. More proof that everything, even air travel, was more fun when you were around.

Joan, you and I first met via satellite. I was six years old when you invited my father and his children—my siblings and me—to appear on your talk show for a Father's Day special. I sat in a studio in London on a live feed to your television studio and proceeded to stick my tongue out, yawn, and scratch my vagina while my dad attempted to explain that we were just a normal family. It was somewhat prophetic, too: At the time, I was still too young to know that the word *vagina* was actually your favorite.

Joan, you were a comedian, international superstar, humanitarian, game changer, mother, and grandmother. You were the hardest-working woman I've ever met in my life (and remember, I was raised by Sharon Osbourne, so this says a lot). Even though you had a mouth like a truck driver, you were the ultimate lady, one of the most gracious and generous people in the world. You were a legend, and you were my best friend.

*Fashion Police* was the best working years of my life, and I know I never told you this, but the reason for that was you, Joan. Every day I woke up excited to go to work because it meant I got to go to work and bask in your humor, wisdom, and light. Even though your daughter, Melissa, our executive producer, was adamant that we not speak to each other or any of the other cohosts during the week in an effort to keep our comments on air spontaneous, you and I found a way around this.

We created secret e-mail accounts from which we wrote back and forth constantly. You were always up so late working and always had to get up so early for work that I don't know if you ever bothered to keep track of time at all! I would wake up every morning to a string of thoughts from you, which meant I was always laughing before I'd even gotten out of bed. When you passed away, it didn't really hit me until that first morning when I woke up and found my secret in-box empty. That is when I more or less stopped checking e-mail entirely.

For most of my life, I thought I had more than enough family (can you blame me?), but when I met you and Missy (which is what we called Melissa), you filled a hole I hadn't even known was there. You were the grandmother and Missy the kind of sister I had never had.

Joan, you were one of the first people, outside of my family, who really, truly believed in me. E! auditioned hundreds of girls for my role on *Fashion Police*, but you said no to every one of them and insisted the producers give it to me. When I had my seizure (spoiler alert! See page 159 for details), you came and visited me in the hospital every single day. I'm pretty sure I'm one of the few people you ever canceled a show for (though I do feel bad about that!). You may have been a workaholic, but there was nothing more important to you than the people you loved, and knowing that made me feel as though I could do anything. You were as loyal as they come, and I've never seen anyone so devoted to her daughter and grandson.

I think everyone needs an older, wiser friend who can give them advice, and you were that for me. You showed me what it was like to work hard, not just for yourself but for the people who depend on you. You would be up all night before the show, shoot in Los Angeles, then get on a plane and fly to New York to do a stand-up show, then turn around and do it all again. You were always the first one at work and the last one to leave, and you never complained about any of it.

You taught me to always remember the names of the people I am working with and that there is no distinction on set—every job was just as important as yours. When one of the writers on *Fashion Police* needed a hip replacement, you gave up your one day off to perform at a benefit show for him. For you, work was something you never took for granted, and you taught me to always remember how lucky we were to even have jobs. "Never give up and never turn down a job," you said, "because you should never think you're too good for something."

You thought it was fabulous to have enemies. If people didn't like you, it meant you were probably doing something to succeed in this world. Every week, you'd ask, "Who do we hate this week?" Then I'd fill you in, and you'd be thrilled and say, "Oh, marvelous!"

You lived by the idea that you should never, ever apologize for who you are. If who you are offends people, then it is because they don't get you, and that's their problem, not yours. You never apologized for who you were or what you said. You stood by it all.

As much fun as it was to watch you make other people laugh, what I loved most was when you cracked yourself up. There would be times when you were laughing so hard at a joke you hadn't even delivered yet that you couldn't get it out.

When I was a guest on your Internet talk show, *In Bed with Joan*, I had no idea that we would be filming from your bed in Melissa's house. In preparation for my arrival, you turned Melissa's laundry room into a green room. It was about the size of a prison cell, and you covered the washer and dryer with these beautiful lace linens and set out a Baccarat bowl filled with candy. When I got to the house, you had your assistant Sabrina walk me in and say, "This is your dressing room," then shut the door behind her when she left.

There wasn't even room for me to sit down, but I didn't know what to say. I'd never been to Melissa's house before, so I didn't want to be rude. I just hopped up on the dryer and waited there. That was when you sent your housekeeper in to dive between my legs to pull clothes out of the dryer and start to do laundry, and then I knew. *Joan's fucking with me right now!* I thought. Sure enough, you were in the next room absolutely pissing yourself.

You were also the only person who knew when I'd had sex. I would say nothing, but I'd walk into work and you'd take one look at me and go, "Oooh, you had sex last night! Tell me everything!"

Poof! I'd go bright red and practically scream, "Oh my god!" but you always managed to get the details from me anyway.

You and I also shared a common trait—we are both nuts about germs! You taught me this trick where, before going in an airplane bathroom, you'd ask the stewardess for a bottle of vodka, then throw it all over the sink and seat to disinfect everything. It made you smell like a boozer, but it definitely worked.

Another thing you did, which worked in your mind, was to take a paper toilet seat cover, place it on the seat, then set it on fire to burn off all the germs. How you weren't setting off fire alarms all over Hollywood, who knew, but you did this once on the set of *Fashion Police* and caught the plastic toilet seat on fire. It melted and shriveled up into a misshapen plastic mass, but the E! budgets being what they were, instead of buying a new one, they just took the toilet seat from the men's room and gave the blokes the burnt one. Soon, the crew were coming to me, asking if they could shit in my dressing room because it hurt their asses to sit on the men's toilet for too long. I'd always say yes and hand over the key.

You always said that the worst thing about getting older was that you ran out of people to whom you could say, "Remember when . . . ?" Well, I can't say that to you anymore, but I am so happy, and so proud, to say that I knew you, a magnificent woman, for twenty-five years and saw you fifty-two weeks a year for six of those.

Now, a note to you, lovely reader: In Joan's honor, as soon as you are finished with this chapter, I want you to shout her favorite word—*vagina*. If you're embarrassed because you're in public or reading somewhere else where you might make a scene, just stop for a second and ask yourself, *What would Joan Rivers do?*

*Love,*
*Kelly O*

# 8 *

## DEAR OZZFEST

You were my sleepaway camp, my stomping ground, my summer school, my traveling circus, and about the most interesting childhood adventure a kid could ever hope to have.

Every summer from birth to when I was almost twenty, I went on tour with my dad. The idea of growing up on a bus might seem like the average person's idea of hell. Yes . . . I had to sleep in a bunk bed that was the size of a coffin. I shared a bathroom about the size of Harry Potter's cupboard under the stairs, with up to twelve people. It may seem impractical to you, as it can only be used to wash your hands or take a piss, because the number one rule on the tour bus is NO SHITTING!

In retrospect, I have probably taken a shit in more truck stop bathrooms than I have in my own bathroom at home! Like they say, what happens on the road stays on the road, and it was a very long road.

Every morning, I woke up in an entirely different state, sometimes even a different country. The Ozzfest crew were the outcasts of society by nothing more than our appearance and love of heavy metal. Ozzfest was, and forever will be, my extended, crazy, loving, dysfunctional, kind, disgusting, generous, heavy metal family.

Ozzfest started in 1996, after Lollapalooza refused to book my dad. They said he wasn't "Lollapalooza material." To that, Mum said, "Fine, fuck you, then," and started her own festival. The first lineup featured eleven bands, including Ozzy Osbourne, Slayer, Danzig, and Sepultura. The next year, it grew to fourteen, adding Black Sabbath, Marilyn Manson, Pantera, and Type O Negative, among others. From the very first show, Ozzfest was a massively huge success.

In my eyes, what made it a success wasn't that it was completely sold out every night, with up to seventy-five thousand people. No, to me it was a success because it gave the metal heads, goths, freaks, and geeks of the world somewhere to belong. Remember the scene from the *Men in Black 2* movie, when Tommy Lee Jones opens the locker and there's a whole new, tiny world? That's what Ozzfest felt like—like you'd stepped into a different universe that most people didn't even know existed, one that had its own gods, customs, and laws.

Before Ozzfest, no one in the music industry really seemed to give a fuck about metal bands or metal fans. Heavy metal is music's eternal outsider. It's not pretty. If you go to a metal show, you're not going to find the popular people. Instead, it's a crowd of glorious misfits who've come together because they all have one thing in common: They fucking love metal. We've all heard someone walk into a room and say, "It smells like sex in here." Walking onto the grounds of Ozzfest was like that, except it was the smell of people's musical dreams coming true. With Ozzfest, metal fans knew that no matter how shit their life was before they came, or how shit it was going to be when they left, they could come to the show, forget about everything, and have the best times of their lives. That joy was contagious, even if you were a miserable teenager, angry at the world like I was.

When Ozzfest came to town, it was like Carnivale had just rolled in. In some cities, it was the biggest thing they'd see all year, with people lined up, cheering and waving along the side of the road as we drove by. The sight was impressive. Each band had a bus and a truck to haul all their equipment, so depending on the tour, there would be anywhere from twenty-five to seventy massive trucks in a giant caravan. It was just like that Coca-Cola commercial where the kids are all excited because "The holidays are coming! The holidays are coming!" We were just like that, except without any fancy lights, just all lit up with insanity.

Now that Dad flies everywhere, I haven't traveled on a tour bus in about fifteen years, but I can still remember that smell. No matter if a bus is brand-new or was built in 1979, they all smell the same: like plastic seats, booze, gasoline, recycled air, and a hint of chemical toilet. No matter what was done to prevent it, it seemed as if extreme things were always happening on and to the buses. One of the buses had an ant infestation like something from another planet, and people couldn't sleep because they'd feel ants crawling through their hair and into their ears.

Another horrible instance will forever be known as "The Tale of the Mystery Log Rider." Trust me, it's a true fable, and to this day it's still a "Who did it?" argument in my household. In short, the cardinal rule was broken: Someone took a dump in the tour bus bathroom. After that, it didn't take long for literal, actual human shit to somehow get sucked into the air vents of our bus. Laws of physics were possibly broken in the process. No one knows how it happened, but we all awoke to the smell of human feces being blown out of the air vents directly onto our faces, and with screams to match.

One thing I loved was the truck stops. They sold velvet paintings, trucker hats (I'm talking real trucker hats, not Von Dutch, or "Von Douche," as I call them), and dream catchers that were made in China. I can't tell you how many jackalopes we bought. (For the uninitiated, a jackalope is a taxidermied jackrabbit with antelope horns and is a mythical creature in the American Southwest.)

As you can imagine, it took a long time for busloads of people to do their business and buy their snacks, so we spent a lot of time at truck stops and got to know several truckers along the way. Ozzfest was a window into one world, and spending more than five minutes at a truck stop was a window into another. I learned what a lot lizard was (for those who don't know, it is a truck stop prostitute) and learned the different numerical codes and slang that truckers would use to signal to one another that there was construction, a car accident, slowed traffic, or cops ahead.

The tour buses had a La-Z-Boy seat, called a jump seat, next to the driver. Usually, this was the place where people would go and sit when they needed to get some work done, but sometimes I'd go and sit there when I was bored on long night drives. When I'd hear the driver's CB radio crackle with things like "10-200" (they need to take a shit on the side of the road) or "10-10 in the wind" (listening and driving), I felt like I was clued in to a secret society. I have a lot of respect for truckers, because they do a really hard job. They deserve more credit for how many accidents they prevent, because if you spend enough time on the highway, you'll see that most people can't drive at all.

Jack, Aimee, and I had a bus to ourselves, which was called the kids' bus no matter how old we were. It was the fun bus, and over the summer, people who we became friends with would slowly migrate to our bus, since it was one of the least disgusting. Aimee, who was in her Post-Adolescent Idealistic Phase, had the back bedroom to herself, and we had to constantly listen to "Nobody Loves Me but You" and "One (Is the Loneliest Number)" on repeat. We were lucky if we got a taste of PJ Harvey. Regardless of her teenage angst, her no-go zone (or as we called it, the Boring Zone) was respected by all. If there is one thing to know about Aimee, it is that nobody fucks with her. (She's my sister, so I know that better than anyone.)

Other than that, everyone kept reminding us that we were free. "You can do whatever you want!" one of our friends encouraged us. "Your parents own the tour!" We were always shocked by this. "No way!" we'd say. "You've seen what Mum and Dad are like when they yell at someone!" We were terrified of that someone being us, so when Mum and Dad gave us a rule—such as being in Dad's dressing room by the time he had finished singing "Paranoid"—we learned the true meaning of humiliation when we didn't comply. Regardless of all this, the truth is that we were naughty little shits, and we took full advantage anyway.

** TRANSLATION

🇬🇧 Port-a-loo
🇺🇸 Porta potty

There was one guy on tour who everyone hated (I won't give any details about him, to save him at least some dignity), and he was always especially obnoxious to Jack and me. When we decided to get revenge, someone threw fireworks into a port-a-loo** right before he went in, so that they were cracking off when he was trying to take a dump. He started yelling and cursing everyone out, but little did he know that the worst was yet to come: me, driving a golf cart.

Everyone was egging me on, of course, so I got the golf cart up to its top speed (which, let's be honest, was probably about seven miles per hour) and rammed it into the side. When he came out, he was covered in shit and that horrible blue disinfecting liquid, and it caused such a mess that my parents had to pay a five-thousand-dollar sanitation cleanup fee. Whoops. Mum ripped me a new one for that.

A lot of the amphitheaters we stopped at had only one road in and one road out, which meant we needed to do a "runner" as soon as the show ended. Everyone would grab a slice of pizza, or whatever else might be considered dinner that night, and book it to the bus, which had a police motorcade waiting to escort us out and around the traffic. Needless to say, if you were the person—like the one and only time I once was—who missed bus call and made the entire tour sit in eight hours of traffic, all because you were off sneaking a Smirnoff Ice behind the bathrooms, you were really and truly fucked!

The inside varied from bus to bus, but typically it had bunks lining the sides. Sometimes, if we were lucky, we'd get a bus with condo bunks, which meant they were tall enough for you to sit up in without knocking your head on the bunk above, but usually they were in stacks of three. This space was your "room," the place you slept for an entire summer, and was basically the size of a body locker in a morgue. Even though they were tiny, some people (definitely not me) still found ways to have sex in these crawl spaces, though I don't even know how they managed to get their ass up and down.

No one ever wanted the bottom bunk, because it was right above the wheels, and you had to be a Zen master to sleep through the rumbling, roaring sound of the tires *kathunk-kathunk*ing as the bus sped down the highway. Some of the guys preferred the top bunk, but I hated having to perform gymnastics and pray for a perfect dismount just so I could hop down to wee, so I usually aimed for the middle.

Every bus had a "junk bunk," which was the empty bed that everyone used for storing their stuff. Because space was so limited on the bus, you had to keep most of your stuff in luggage compartments underneath, which was a giant pain in the ass. If you left anything you needed in your bag, you couldn't get it until the next stop, which would sometimes be hours away. At the beginning of tour, everyone was really good at keeping only what they needed in the bus, scared that they'd just end up having to move anything they stashed in the junk bunk. But as the summer wore on, people grew more confident—thinking, *No one's going to use this*—and the junk bunk would fill to the brim with the random shit everyone stashed and forgot about. Inevitably, there would come a night when an extra person needed to sleep on your bus, and then you'd have to clean six months' worth of who knows what out of there, usually at some ungodly hour in the morning, so that they could go to bed.

As we traveled from show to show, I'd look through the tour book, which had a map of our route. The longest leg we'd ever do was twenty-seven hours, driving from Seattle to somewhere in Texas. On rides like those, or just any time things were getting pretty rank, we'd have to clear out our junk bunk to make room for a second driver, who would get flown in so the drivers could each take shifts and we would not have to stop.

While Jack and I were just as terrified of going against the bosses (Mum and Dad) as everybody else on tour, there were obvious perks of being Ozzy's kids, the main one being that we got second choice of where our bus parked. Therefore, we never parked anywhere near the second stage.

Second-stage show sound checks started at eight A.M. If you had the misfortune of being parked nearby, you would be awoken, after having gone to bed just a few hours before, to the not-so-sweet sounds of sound check—the double-kick drum going *berrderdadadadadadderderderderder*, accompanied by the soothing vocals of the microphone checks . . . "Testing, testing, one, two, three . . ." Over and over again.

Even if you were parked so far away from the second stage that the kick drum was just a whisper in the distance, wafts of parking lot barbecue drifted past the blackout curtain and into your bunk to tell your nose it was time to get up. This was the smell of people tailgating, pounding cheap beer early in the morning and grilling meat on the engines of their cars—the smell of people getting ready to have a really good time.

The second stage was usually smaller bands, and in the beginning, there was always a hierarchy on tour between the main stage bands, the second stage bands, and the carnies. The roadies were always cautioning my brother and me to stay away from the Freak Show, who was part of the Village of the Damned that toured with us, but those quickly became our favorite people. In our opinion, the Freak Show was the best place to be. We wanted to hang out with the two-legged dog who walked upright like a human and who we tried to adopt (but her owner was too in love and wouldn't let us) and with Reverend B. Dangerous, who would let us use an electric screwdriver or hammer nails into his nose. After a while, it became normal for Jack and me to spend our afternoons being called onstage to staple an ace of spades to someone's ball sack.

Through our drifting about, from the main stage to the Freak Show to the second stage and everywhere in between, we eventually broke down the barriers and brought all the different bands and camps together. Everyone got along so well that we became a family, and if there was one band of assholes that came on the tour, it became a toxic environment for the whole lot. You'd see the biggest, gnarliest, ugliest grown death metal men upset because they'd just seen some dick be rude to an assistant. This taught me so much about treating everyone as equals.

Over the years, we did have a few epic pricks on tour, especially the lead singer from Lostprophets, who creeped me out from day one. He had the most plaque-covered teeth I have ever seen. He looked at people as if they were food, and he had an evil appetite that could not be filled. He was uncomfortably nice, in a way that told me instantly the he had something big to hide.

I was spot on, unfortunately. He was finally revealed to be a massive, hard-core pedophile. I don't know what I would do if I ever saw him again, because his crimes are some of the worst things I have ever heard. So I guess it is fortunate for him, and for the rest of us, that he is probably going to be in jail for the rest of his miserable life.

But for the most part, we remained one great big happy rock 'n' roll juggernaut. Bands like Pantera, Slipknot, Linkin Park, and System of a Down looked out for Jack and me like we were their own siblings. At the same time, they didn't hide anything from us or treat us like stupid little kids. Phil from Pantera showed me how to mix Sprite and Crown Royal, and he even let me keep the fancy purple bag the bottle came in. I still count Mikey from Incubus as one of my best friends in the whole world, and when it came time for me to record my own album, he and José were the ones who gave me the confidence to sing in a studio for the first time. They actually produced and played all the instrumentals for my first single, "Papa Don't Preach."

Marilyn Manson never seemed to forget that we were still kids. He kept us entertained by giving us weird presents or telling strange stories. One of his gifts was a packet of this tasteless herbal powder you could slip in someone's drink and make them shit their pants.

Ironically, it was usually the groupies, who weren't even part of the tour, who were the rudest to Jack and me, probably because treating us like shit was some fucked-up way for them to convince themselves that they weren't only there to hang around with rock stars and give blow jobs. (Allow me to paint you a picture: In order to get access to the rock stars, one first has to get through parking lot security, backstage security, a roadie who would then make an introduction to the tour manager, and then the band. So how many dicks is that? I'm counting at least four before walking through the backstage door.) Well, after we had that powder, anyone who was a bitch to us had to watch—and most likely wash—her ass.

My friends now might wonder why I'm single and don't trust men, but they need only look back to my time on tour to understand why: The dynamic between the groupies and the bands was disgusting. I must have seen at least one hundred dicks being sucked before I ever saw a penis that was meant for my eyes only. It wasn't unusual to walk in on someone in the middle of the act. Everyone just did their best to ignore it and walk off.

I once saw a girl stick a pen up her ass and use it to write people's names. There was the girl who was convinced to take off all her clothes and do naked jumping jacks while chanting, "I love Ozzy! I love Ozzy!" just so that she could get a free glow stick. A fucking glow stick!

Then there was the one who had "Brown-Eyed Girl" tattooed around her asshole—though, to her credit, she had a very cute anus. One of the nicest assholes I have ever seen, that's for sure, and it was a really well-done tattoo.

At the end of every tour, Mum would throw a party that was out of control. Jack and I were always up front, no matter what the "entertainment" was—strippers, porn stars, freaky clowns, fire eaters, everything. I saw a stripper fuck a lollipop and then give it to my manny (male nanny) to suck on. Another one lay on her back and dumped an entire two-liter bottle of water up her gearbox,** stood up, then bent over and sprayed the crowd. The spray hit me, and I started screaming bloody murder. Dad ran over, hooked me under one arm, and then hauled me to the bathroom and shoved me in the shower with all my clothes on.

** TRANSLATION

🇬🇧 Gearbox
🇺🇸 Vagina

The cherry on the cake, and the most disgusting thing I ever saw, was a pregnant woman shooting her breast milk into people's mouths for backstage entertainment. I was standing next to a friend of mine, and we were watching in horror, when my friend started to retch uncontrollably. It was that gagging sound that a cat makes when it's about to spit up a hairball: *gaaaawwwwwwwthhuuuccckkkk, gaaaawwwwwwwthhuuuccckkkk* . . . As soon as I heard him, I also started to gag, and we ran out of the room, dying with laughter but also scared that we were going to start puking any minute.

Far be it from me to slut-shame, but try being the daughter of a rock star and watching groupies disrespect your mum by throwing themselves at your father and any male within his radius. When you are looking at it from that perspective, it is hard to see using your vagina to gain access to a rock star as an act of empowerment.

As you can imagine, when I wasn't able to bring a friend on tour, I was pretty starved for female friendship. When Marilyn started dating Dita Von Teese, it was like the heavens had opened up and sent us an angel. She was the first true lady, aside from my mum, that I'd ever met on tour. Dita was the furthest thing from a groupie. I thought she was the most beautiful woman I'd ever seen. In fact, I still do.

I grew up such a tomboy that I'm still learning how to do girly shit, but everything that I do know, I learned from Dita and drag queens. I would try to make myself invisible and just stare at her, taking mental notes on how she walked, how she held her champagne glass, and how she never, ever walked around looking like shit. Meanwhile, I might have been wearing my brother's shirt and my mum's skirt, because that was all I could find in the junk bunk that morning.

Dita and I are still friends, and while I will never be as girly or as graceful as she is, she did teach me that I have it in me to search for those qualities. I'll always be grateful to her for that.

The summer that Limp Bizkit was on the main stage for the first time, Fred Durst came onstage by jumping out of a thirty-foot-tall Styrofoam toilet. Getting that toilet in and out of certain amphitheaters was the nightmare of the tour, but when Fred couldn't have his toilet, he would lose his fucking shit. (I think I would, too.)

One band, which shall not be named, brought an entire gym with them. It required an additional roadie whose sole responsibility was to set it up for them, over and over, with each relocation. It even had carpeting, which was made more disgusting by the copious amounts of body oil they would be rubbing all over one another when off-shift from pumping iron and running on the treadmill. Initially, this scene was jaw-droppingly shocking, but it quickly became the biggest joke of the tour and a source of entertainment. That shit was way better than television.

I remember walking by it with Mum, who'd had to help them figure out the logistics, and she just said, "Fucking pussies," under her breath. This was a metal tour. No matter how much money they made, most of the bands probably could have survived on Budweiser and slept in a trash can if they had to, but this particular band was out there in MAC Studio Fix powder, even when we were in Arizona and it was 125 degrees.

One year, Dad decided he wanted his own Jumbotron. After much debate about paying to rent one for the entire length of each tour or buying one to have forever, Mum and Dad decided to buy one. It was so huge, it required its own truck. Only a few weeks later, the driver decided to pick up a lot lizard and apparently she shifted his stick just a little too hard. When he pulled his O face, the truck got wrecked and Dad's shiny new purchase got wrecked right along with it. The police found the truck driver walking down the side of the highway, stark-ass naked.

After being on tour for so many years, I started to develop a sixth sense about the new bands who joined. I could tell who was going to be big, who was going to fizzle out, who was going to get fired, and who was going to end up addicted to drugs. I learned a lot of it from watching Mum, who always seemed to be one step ahead of everyone else in the music industry. She saw the genius in Queens of the Stone

Age and put them on the main stage before anyone else even really knew who they were. They were a real band's band, and when word spread that they were coming on tour, everyone was so excited.

When my mum was booking new bands, she would always ask Jack and me a lot of questions about what we liked and who we were into. I didn't realize it at the time, but this was her way of doing research. Rock 'n' roll is passed down from father to son, from mother to daughter; it is generationless. However, she was always looking for the next big thing, and it was really important to her that Ozzfest appealed to audiences of all ages.

My mum was badass before it was trendy for a woman to be a badass. She just wasn't someone you would fuck with, *ever*. She had everything on lock. She didn't just oversee the entire tour—she paid attention to every single detail of it and knew everyone's name. For example, at every new venue, she ordered more port-a-loos and placed them between the beer tents and the merch stands, knowing that most smaller bands made a lot of their money from selling T-shirts. Another time, there was a tornado warning at one of the shows. I remember huddling underneath the stage with Mum at the open-air amphitheater while she was on the phone with the fire marshal, screaming at him to allow more people to join us so they could be out of harm's way. "What about everyone out there?" she kept asking. Luckily, the tornado didn't hit and everyone was safe.

It often seemed like there were no rules on Ozzfest, but there was one big one—unofficial and unwritten—and it was law: No one ever disrespected Mum or Dad. They weren't just the bosses—they were the tour parents. Anyone, no matter how big or small their job was, could go to Mum with a problem and know that she would do her best to fix it.

This rule was broken in a major way in 2005, when Iron Maiden was on tour. Iron Maiden is a talented group and everyone I met in the band was lovely . . . but there's always one bad egg. For some reason, the lead singer, Bruce Dickinson, who was a little, Napoleon-complex of a man, had it out for my dad.

Every night, he'd peacock onstage, talking about how he didn't need a reality show to stay relevant, how he didn't need a jet because he flew his own plane here, and how he wasn't coming out here just to sing karaoke. All of those were jabs at my dad, and it was mental, especially since Iron Maiden were opening for Ozzy Osbourne, so let me just put this very bluntly: My dad was basically paying his bills.

Dad has written or cowritten all his songs, and has been singing them for decades, but he's like me. We are both extremely dyslexic. Sometimes all it takes is a sudden sound or flash to distract him and make him lose his train of thought. For that reason, he had a monitor at the bottom of the stage that scrolled the lyrics, so that if something did ever happen in the middle of a song, he could pick up where he left off without a hiccup. The prompter is there just in case—if you watch my dad perform, you'll see he never even looks at it, and most people never even know it's there.

But Bruce had to talk about it, even though Iron Maiden were getting paid plenty of money to be on Ozzfest, and since we are being honest, at that time, he hardly had anywhere else to be. To me, it felt like Bruce had had a problem with my dad since they were kids, probably because Black Sabbath was more successful. Regardless of the reasoning, it was petty. The one thing that stood out to me was that, after years and years of spineless jabs from Bruce, my father never once responded and always took the high road. He had no problem with Bruce, and since he was always backstage getting ready when

Iron Maiden was performing, he didn't even really know what was going on.

By the end of the tour, I had had enough of this fucking cunt going onstage and talking about my family every night. Pretty much everyone else on tour were sick of it, too. It all came to a head at our show in San Bernardino. The highest access you could have on tour was a skull pass. A skull pass meant you could go absolutely anywhere. If there was a fence in your way, someone had better move it. I made a bargain with a friend of mine who worked for one of the tour sponsors: I'd get him a skull pass if he took the blame for what we were about to do. He agreed.

I asked my mum to order eggs and not to ask any questions. God only knows why, but she did it. What must have been three thousand eggs got delivered to me in under an hour. I rounded up everyone I could—all our friends, production, and even band members from the first and second stages. We all had black hoodies and bandannas around our faces, and we looked like we were about to rob somebody. Instead, we loaded up our pockets with eggs and baby powder. I had on a giant fanny pack with thirty-five eggs in it. I remember the specific number because I had counted to see how many would fit.

As soon as we were ready, we funneled down to the photography pit, a line of open space between the stage and the crowd. Security was shitting themselves. We were clearly up to no good, but every person in the group had a skull pass around their neck, which meant we were unstoppable.

For the first song of Iron Maiden's set, we all stood with our backs to the stage, which meant Bruce was singing to a first few rows filled with the backs of a bunch of heads, all wearing black. Our cue was their second song, which was usually right when Bruce would start taking digs at my dad. The minute they started, we all spun around and emptied our pockets, throwing eggs and powder. I hit Bruce right in the face with an egg. Now, I've never been athletic, but something came over me that day and I'm still impressed with my aim.

As soon as security and the crowd started to catch on to what was happening, we spread like wildfire and ran backstage where no one could catch us. It was our *Sandlot* moment, the triumphant, egg-throwing end to a summer of carnies, groupies, two-legged dogs, and a whole lot more innocent, heavy metal fun.

I'm not being sarcastic—it really was innocent, and there were innocent times, too. For example, if a band like Incubus was on tour and knew we were headed to a particularly beautiful venue, such as the Gorge in Seattle or Red Rocks in Colorado, they'd push everyone so we could get there early and watch the sun slip up over the horizon.

It was magic watching the crew build and then dismantle a whole new world each and every day. There were superheroes, like Rigger Dan, who would free climb up the jib to check out the lights. You had to be a special kind of brave to be a rigger in those days, because who knew when the last time the stage was really, truly safety-checked? Dan had previously been a porn star and had also lost a finger after being bitten by a rattlesnake. He was so much fun, and one of the greatest guys ever.

When the shows were over and the crowds were clearing out, Jack and I would head out into the field to see what we could find. It wasn't like a Justin Bieber concert, where you'd find a few lip glosses and some chewed gum. We'd find tomahawks, dead animals, and enough bandannas to outfit several Boy Scout troops. Sometimes there would be scorched patches of grass where someone had set the earth on fire, or we'd find wallets and keys to Porsches or Mercedeses. We turned that stuff in. The tomahawks, we kept.

A lot of the band members were only a few years older than Jack and me, and we were all just looking to have fun. If you were close to our age, you were accepted as part of the crew. You were supported. People believed in you and no one shat on you about who you were or who you wanted to be. To an outsider, Ozzfest might seem shocking, but for me, I was more shocked when I went into the rest of the world. There, I couldn't believe how unaccepting people were, and how vitriolic they could be to someone who was different. To this day, I will gravitate toward the freaks wherever I am, because that's what I am. That's who I am. And I have Ozzfest to thank for that!

*Love,*
*Kelly O*

# 9 *

# DEAR LONDON

You have always been my true home. That is why when I was nineteen, I decided to move back to you to live on my own. That was also when I really fell head over stiletto heels in love with the city. The next few years that I lived there were some of the happiest of my life, and moving back was probably one of the best decisions I ever made.

It was also one of the toughest because it was the first time that I had ever left my family behind. At the time, the *Osbournes* TV show had ended and Mum's cancer was in full remission.

After spending so much time looking after someone else, I knew it was time to look after me, and I knew I needed to get away. I'd been so focused on being a daughter that I'd neglected being a person, and while I don't regret that for one second, I knew that is no way to spend the rest of my life. I had to claim my independence. I needed to make my own mistakes and figure out who I was outside my family, and time to just be whatever the fuck it was I thought I wanted to be. Also, I needed to find a way to stop self-medicating.

Painkillers had become my crutch, as they don't only kill your physical pain; they kill your mental pain, too. After a few years of using them to stun my misery, I was a full-blown addict and knew that I would have a much harder time getting Vicodin in England because at that time, medication like that was not available outside of a hospital. Addicts in the UK were different as a result of that inaccessibility. There, people would go from drinking to shooting heroin because they couldn't get their hands on anything in between. I'm not saying that's a good thing, or that I had any intentions of going stone-cold sober, just that I thought that moving to London would put some distance between me and the drugs I'd become dependent on—otherwise known as my DOC**—so off I went.

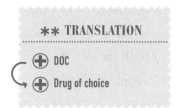

**✱✱ TRANSLATION**

➕ DOC
➕ Drug of choice

My two childhood best friends, Sammy and Fleur, lived in London, and I also knew people like Kate Moss and Lee Starkey. London is a very tight-knit city, so with just two childhood mates to go to the pub with and a few acquaintances to invite me out, it soon felt like I knew everyone. For the first time ever, I had a group of friends of my own who didn't know my family. If people expected me to be a twat, all it took to win them over was the fact that I wasn't. People have a much better bullshit detector in London, so it wasn't hard to make mates. They saw me for me, and because of that, I started to see myself that way as well.

One of the best friends I made was Omar, who came over to my first apartment, a sublet in St. John's Wood, one night with my friend

Margot. I was tripping on ecstasy that must have been cut with acid, because I was wearing a classic yellow raincoat and making snow angels on the floor of my flat,** thinking I was covered with water in my own apartment. I looked at Omar and said, "It's raining." He must have thought I was batshit crazy, but not crazy enough to leave, and he basically moved in that night and never left.

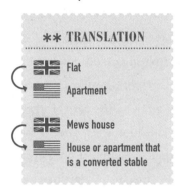

** TRANSLATION

🏴󠁧󠁢󠁥󠁮󠁧󠁿 Flat
🇺🇸 Apartment

🏴󠁧󠁢󠁥󠁮󠁧󠁿 Mews house
🇺🇸 House or apartment that is a converted stable

Shortly thereafter, we moved into a new place. It was a mews house** with three stories. My bedroom was on the top floor, there were two spares on the second floor, and the kitchen and living room were on the first. Extra space meant room for extra people, and when I found out that friends of mine were recording an album and trying to find a place to live off the measly allowance of five pounds a day per person from their record company, I invited them to come stay at mine. Having a whole band sleeping in the living room was completely normal for someone who'd grown up on a tour bus. Unlike the dysfunctional family I'd grown up with, this ragtag group of assholes became the dysfunctional family I chose. Over the years, if you were my friend, it became known that if you were in town, you had a place to stay and that place was mine. I had everyone from Naomi Campbell, artist Alex Prager, designer Kim Jones, Amy Winehouse, John Galliano, the Like, and various other bands stay with me.

People always assume that us Osbournes were trust-fund kids, but that could not be further from the truth. From day one, Mum and Dad made it very clear that we had to be self-sufficient and that they would not support us after a certain age. Lucky enough for me, I have been self-sufficient since I was fifteen. I had to pay my mortgage, so I had to keep working. Sometimes that went well—I was the youngest person to ever play Mama Morton in *Chicago* on the West End** and got my first TV fashion gig as the host of *Project Catwalk*.

** TRANSLATION

West End

The Broadway of London

Other times it didn't go as well. I hosted a radio show for the BBC called *The Sunday Night Surgery*, took lots of various TV hosting gigs, and got fired a lot. I showed up to work hungover, I was late, or I would think that I could sneak out a few hours early, forgetting that without my chatting, someone would go, "It's gone a bit quiet in here, hasn't it? Wait . . . Where the fuck is Kelly?!" I once even got written up at the BBC for showing up to work in my pajamas too many times, even though it was radio and my show aired from eleven to midnight. I also got written up another time for talking about pizza too much while on the air.

Before you write me off as some entitled prick who couldn't hold a job, let me remind you that I was twenty years old! Find me a twenty-year-old who doesn't think it's more fun to hang out with her friends than go to work. And yes, maybe I got there a few (or forty) minutes late, or left a few (or ninety) minutes early, but no matter what state I was in, I showed up and I was always prepared.

The worst instance of this was when my family and I hosted the Brit Awards in 2008. I'd gotten the schedule wrong and thought I only had to show up at eight A.M. for rehearsal, and that after that, I'd get a few hours to sleep it off in my dressing room. After being out all night with the Klaxons, I showed up at eight A.M. to find out that this wasn't just a rehearsal and there was no downtime—it was show time from the minute I walked in.

The whole day felt like having food poisoning in a place where you can't take a shit. I started to have cold sweats and panic, wondering how I was going to get through the day, while simultaneously being terrified that my parents would see right through me. Even though I am far from what you would call religious, I found myself bargaining with God: "Dear God, if you just let me get through this day alive and without puking in front of a live audience, I promise I'll never drink again . . ." Then I gave up on bothering to ask God to save me and just started praying for him to kill me, swiftly and suddenly. I felt faint and started to realize that the only way I would get through it was the hair of the dog.

What I realized in moments like this, when I was forced to compensate for the fact that I felt like dog shit on the inside by being extra professional on the outside, was that I was actually somehow pulling it off and truly being professional. Which was exactly the case that day. I tried to keep it together, but anyone backstage who had been with me the night before would point and laugh, reminding me of my misery—as if it were even possible to forget. This all went on as I sat next to my mother under a blinding spotlight, squinting to read the teleprompter. To this day, I don't know how my mum didn't pick up on what was going on.

By the time the awards show was over, I'd been awake for almost forty-eight hours, and it was the first time in my life I'd ever pulled a proper all-nighter. Once the show ended, I made it to the after party for long enough to finally have that one drink, and then I went straight home, where my roommates were just rallying to go out.

Whenever I had to work, I'd call home to my roommates about twenty times during the day to see what I was missing out on. More than likely, they would be asleep, but on the day of the Brit Awards, I was seeking moral support for the state I had managed to get myself in. Whenever I got paid, the whole house was excited, because my having money meant we were all going out that night with whatever was left over after paying the bills.

Aside from Omar, it was Jay, who managed one of the bands that lived with me, who exhibited any sense of responsibility. They were the only two, aside from me, who ever cleaned. On the rare occasion that we decided to stay in, Omar would cook, but it took so bloody long that by the time he finished, we were all mullered.** No one ended up eating except for me because (a) Omar's cooking was amazing, and (b) I never turn down a good meal.

About once a week or so, one of us would have the grand idea to have a movie night. "Oh, we're going to stay in and watch *Overboard*," we'd say when we invited everyone over, and then it never, ever happened. I can't remember a single night that we stayed in.

There was always something enticing happening in London. Like a party in Shoreditch where Björk was playing on the roof of a garage, where I got split off from everyone and somehow spent the whole night hanging out with a lady named Shoplifter, who made all Björk's wigs, and Björk herself. Who would have wanted to miss all that?

There was no such thing as a regular night for us, but we did have a few regular haunts. The Columbia Hotel had a somewhat glamorous reputation because that was where bands used to stay back in the day. You'd always run into Canadian or Japanese tourists in the hallway, desperately seeking rock stars, but to me, the Columbia was a first-rate shithole.

To get a drink, you'd go downstairs and ring a bell, and an old woman would come from around the corner in an apron. It would go something like this:

"Well, what do you want?" she'd ask, while giving you a look like she'd prefer you just die right there and then.

"Please may I have a vodka cranberry and orange and a packet of crisps?"**

** TRANSLATION

Packet of crisps

Bag of potato chips

Her disdain for my politeness only made her yearn all the more for my imminent death. She would slam a cup down on the counter and put one single ice cube in it, if I was lucky. It was always only one single cube, like ice was some luxury that had to be rationed. By the time she finished pouring, the beverage was still warm as fuck, with a little water for good measure, thanks to how fast that one ice cube melted before I even took the first sip.

The Columbia was aptly named, because back then the amount of cocaine consumed there was probably keeping several cartels in business. It was the first place I'd ever seen people do coke right out in the open. The hotel was closing soon for renovations, and I guess people took that as license to cease giving any fucks at all, when there weren't that many given in the first place.

The new hotel that rose to take its place was in Shepherd's Bush, the K West. To me, it was also a miserable shithole, although it gave the illusion that it was grand by the choice of décor. As my father always says, "You can't paint a turd white. It's still a turd." The whole place always smelled like a swimming pool, probably from all the bleach they used to swab it down. One of the rooms we once stayed in had a bullet hole in the window. However, the K West was close to Heathrow and the BBC TV studios, so bands would stay there when they came to town, and inevitably, we'd end up there as well. We actually didn't know any better—we thought it was really posh at the time.

Some nights we would find ourselves in random situations, like when we ended up at the Pogues' front man Shane MacGowan's birthday party at the Boogaloo, where he slept through the entire thing and someone had set up a velvet rope around him like he was some sort of museum exhibition. I'll give the guy a break, as it *was* his birthday, and call it performance art. When the birthday cake came out for him, he woke up just long enough to punch it and then smash it all over his face. I guess he had a happy birthday.

** TRANSLATION

Tesco
A big grocery store chain in the UK

Weird in a good way was when you'd find a handwritten flyer in Notting Hill that just read "TESCO** DISCO TONIGHT." Tesco Disco was fucking legendary, even though it was just someone's flat next to a Tesco, where the bartender made you drinks at the kitchen table. It would open up after all the pubs had closed and was eventually shut down by the police, which was no surprise to anyone, since everything about it was illegal.

In my scene, there were a few people who did smack, but they were so strung-out that my heart was always breaking for them. There were also more than a few people who did cocaine, which ended up on the List of Banned Substances for Kelly by my friends, because it would only make me tired, or "boring," as they'd put it. You would always hear someone yelling, "Don't give any to Kelly. She'll just fall asleep!"

The funny thing is that I don't even recall ever asking for coke. Plus, the first thing you have to do after snorting a line is take a shit, and taking a shit at a someone else's house or a club is definitely not a party trick.

We were always at Bungalow 8, which was a tiny spot tucked inside the St Martins Lane Hotel and down a steep set of stairs. I was always falling on my ass going down those stairs, but I would just get back up and carry on. I wasn't the only one—at least four times a night, you'd hear a scream, followed by a series of thuds, and know exactly what had just happened.

Most of my mates lived in Camden, and even though that wasn't my neighborhood, the Hawley Arms became my local. It was a bit of a shithole, but the best kind of shithole—when you had to go for a wee, you'd get the key and go up to the owner's apartment, which was right above the bar. My friends and I were always the only people in there and could do whatever we wanted. Amy Winehouse was our mischievous ringleader. If Amy said to do something, people would do it, and she'd easily convince someone to let us have a lock in after closing hours, or step behind the bar to start serving drinks herself.

The paps are ruthless in England, and I was often with people they considered prime prey, like Kate Moss, Amy, Nick Grimshaw, or Alexa Chung. In California, there are laws that the paparazzi have to stay several yards away from you, but in London, you're fair game. Often, they'd work in teams and chase you down on motocross bikes.

One would come right in front of you and start flashing the camera in your face so you couldn't see what was happening, and the other would duck in front so they could get a shot up your skirt.

We didn't understand why they always seemed to know where we were going before we'd even get there—or why stories that seemed fabricated contained one true detail—but it all made sense later when we found out that *News of the World* was hacking everyone's phone. This also explained the time I was at Grimmy's house when someone knocked on the door to tell us he thought we were being hacked. Sure enough, across the street was a bloke sitting in his car on a laptop. Not strange at all, right? When we decided to walk by and have a look at what he was doing, he switched the screen to porn as soon as we got close.

If it was getting too hectic to be out, we'd go to Club Kitchen—which meant going to someone's flat or house and just hanging out in their kitchen. Often, we'd race back to mine, where the gate meant that the paparazzi had to at least keep some distance and couldn't creep right up to the door. This resulted in a few unintentional slumber parties, because if they saw us go in, they'd camp out and wait for us to emerge. Everyone would spend the night to make sure we weren't giving them what they wanted.

The next day, we'd have a good laugh at the reporting of the drug-fueled night of partying that had happened at my place, because the reality was that we'd stayed up till dawn reenacting episodes of *Will & Grace* after Omar had printed out the scripts off the Internet.

**\*\* TRANSLATION**

Fuck all

Absolutely nothing

The jobs I did have always paid very late, and all my mates were in bands and didn't have fuck all,** either, so many of our plans were dictated by where we thought we could get free drinks. When no one was having a party or we couldn't find a bartender we knew, we'd get creative. One such scheme that I invented involved me taking one of the awards I had won and shoving it into my largest handbag, as if I had just won the award that night and we were celebrating. Someone would always offer to buy us a round of drinks, we'd take it, thank them profusely, then head on to the next pub to continue our manipulative celebration.

As you may know, there are no dollar bills in London—only pound coins. What is considered pocket change in the US could be as much as twenty quid in the UK. At some point in the night, we'd all dig through our pockets and pool our money in the center of the table to see if we had enough to get a bite at Wagamama. Upon reflection, I wish I hadn't been too proud to just ask my parents for money, if I was really that hungry for food.

I never went so far as to feel normal, but these few years in London were the most free I've ever felt. This was pre-Uber, and black cabs in London were so expensive. Public transportation became my best friend. I got everywhere by taking the tube and the bus, just like every other Londoner, and I had tube maps and bus routes memorized.

Regardless of what mode of transportation we used to get somewhere, our feet almost always took us home. Inevitably, no matter how much we'd planned not to, my mates and I would miss the last tube or bus. Due to the number of people in our group, Addison Lee** was not an option, and we'd have to walk to our next destination. Omar almost always led the way. He knew the backstreets and shortcuts of

** TRANSLATION

Addison Lee

The original taxi company in the UK, otherwise known as "Addy Lee"

London better than most cabbies. He could turn a half-hour walk into ten minutes by cutting through some alley, but he also always made everyone walk at his pace. By the time we'd get to wherever we were going, I'd be clammy and sweaty and have to duck into the loo to redo my hair and makeup. On some nights, if we got really desperate, we'd take a bicycle tuk-tuk, which always made me have an attack of guilt. *Is this really bad that we're paying someone to pedal us home?* I'd ask myself, as the guys next to me laughed and screamed and didn't think anything of it. *Is this slave labor?*

That was such a special time for me in London, but I think it was a rare and special time in general, and I'm so thankful I got to be a part of it. Almost all my friends were in bands or involved in music, and on any given night, we'd go see the Arctic Monkeys, the Horrors, the Klaxons, the Libertines, the Rascals, Amy, or any number of people who were truly talented. These were bands who were very young, played their own instruments, were writing their own music—that was good!—and weren't manufactured, and this kind of scene hadn't happened in London in a very long time. We didn't know it was anything unusual, though—it was just our lives. We were just kids trying to establish our friendships and figure out what to do next.

I remember once talking to Princess Beatrice in the powder room at one of Elton John's parties, and she told me how she'd gotten grounded for taking the tube. Everyone who has to take the tube in London hates it, but that was all she wanted to do: buy a ticket and take a ride like everyone else out there.

This is why I'm so thankful for my time in London. I didn't always go to bed happy, but I almost always woke up that way, excited about my life rather than hating it. I still wasn't totally sober, and I still fucked up all the time, but the mistakes that I was making were 100 percent mine. I can look back at that time and own up to the fact that I was irresponsible and an asshole, and rather than blaming someone else for my behavior, I know it was all me. I'm grateful that I got a chance to get it out of my system. Rather than feeling trapped by who I was, I started to appreciate it. I still didn't completely like myself in those years, but I was starting to think that maybe someday I would . . .

 *Love,*
*Kelly O*

# 10 *

······································································································

# DEAR CHATEAU MARMONT

Are you a cunt, or am I?

You sure did begin with grand intentions, and I bet you were never meant to become what you are today: a playground for the modern-day self-proclaimed Hollywood Antidisestablishmentarianists—otherwise known as Beverly Hills kids with Los Feliz attitudes.

But that's what you've become, and if I hear one more malnourished It Girl go, "Oh my God, let's go to the Chateau! Their Bolognese is like sooooooo good!" I'm going to poke my fucking eyeballs out.

First of all, the Bolognese is shit. Mediocre at best.

Second, judging from the slender physiques of many of your patrons and their inability to shut the fuck up . . . no one is going to the Chateau to eat!

However, the Chateau does serve a purpose as a balm that douchebags use to soothe their social inadequacies, and so that's why I tend to stay far away.

As I write this, though, I'm actually sitting at the Chateau, awestruck by its contradictions. It's a beautiful, fairy-tale building that holds more romantic, tragic history than anyplace else in Hollywood. This is the place where Led Zeppelin rode their motorcycles through the lobby, James Dean jumped through a window, Jim Morrison fell from a drainpipe, John Belushi OD'd, and Helmut Newton died after crashing his Cadillac into a wall. For these reasons and more, it's a top tourist attraction, provided that the tourists can actually get past the entrance to the valet.

So as I'm sitting here, I'm wondering why people are so attracted to this place, myself included, because as much as I say I hate it and hate myself when I'm here, I keep coming back, and so I decided to indulge in one of my favorite hobbies: eavesdropping. I started listening in on other people's conversations.

Here are just a few things I heard. Please keep in mind that it was more than half empty, and on a Saturday.

- "It's like, so like, transcendent."

  *The only thing transcendent about the man saying this was his hairline, and I seriously question if he even knows what* transcendent *means.*

- "It would be so cool if we could shoot in Paris. Let's do it in Paris. But who's gonna pay for it? I mean, the actors will just have to work for free, hahahahaha. I will just ask my dad to pay for it. Cheers, we are going to Paris . . . Like, can I get another Bellini?"

*This girl was basically having a conversation with herself while the other people at her table never had a chance to respond. I hope her dad has a big bank account.*

- "Soooooo, how do you get Kanye in London?"

  *Apparently, the guy saying this doesn't understand basic principles of economics and travel. You pay him and put him on an airplane.*

- "Are you a producer?"

  *. . . someone asked the waitress.*

- "What about Sundance? They make amazing films. Will there be subtitles? I don't do subtitles."

  *Sundance doesn't make films, they screen them. Plus, unless you want to avoid the international markets entirely, you're going to have subtitles. Her ignorance is not bliss.*

- "Almost like a dream sequence, you know?"

  *I have no idea, but this morning is starting to feel like one.*

- "I made a character for myself where you will shoot me all over LA. Just me and my photography."

  *Isn't that you just being you? That is not a character, but it is incredibly narcissistic.*

. . .

I started to sweat and feel physically sick. Nothing anyone was saying made one bit of sense. It was all psychobabble bullshit. What was I even doing here in the first place?

Then all of a sudden, a girl in a wheelchair came up to me and asked if she could pet my dog. There was something about her demeanor that instantly made me feel comfortable, so I asked her and her friend to come join us. After a few minutes of awkward conversation, we really struck up a friendship. She told me her life story (which was pretty fucking amazing): Long story short, she was born to a drug addict mother and later adopted by a Buddhist lesbian couple. She grew up in a Buddhist colony in San Francisco but moved to Los Angeles for work. She was working two jobs, one in TV and another as an intern for a social media company.

I asked her, "If you could only pick one thing you would love to do for fun that you haven't done since moving here, what would it be?"

Her response broke my heart—what she wanted to do most of all was something that I 100 percent take for granted. She just wanted to go to a Hollywood club and go dancing, but she hadn't because they all turned her away at the door.

Her story infuriated me and lit a fire under my ass. How can people be so cruel? I made a couple of calls to my good friend Brian, who runs Giorgio's at the Standard, and within an hour she was on the list and looking forward to her first Hollywood club experience. I don't think that I have ever seen so much excitement on one person's face. Which got me thinking.

Chateau, maybe you're not the Shiteau Marmont after all. Though it might seem like they are few and far between, there are good people in this world, and you can find them anywhere. So maybe I should stop being such a judgmental cunt, and just order the fucking Bolognese.

*Love,*
*Kelly O*

# 11 *

························································································

# DEAR FRIENDS

Everyone knows that you can't pick your family, but you can pick
your friends. And please note that when I say *friends,* I mean the real
ones who are in the flesh, who are there for you no matter what, not
the usernames that like your photos on social media.

In Los Angeles, it's very easy to figure out who your real friends
are. All you have to do is ask them one question: "Can you take me to
the airport?" This separates the real friends from the fake very fast. If
you've spent any time in LA and are no longer blinded by the bright
lights of bullshit, you know what I am talking about. It's called the
City of Lost Angels, for fuck's sake. It's also where lost angels go to
die, but I digress. Almost everyone in LA is either between jobs or
lucky enough to have a job but most likely has some strange version of
employment that doesn't require them to be present between nine and
five. Many of them are just at home waiting until it's time to start

getting ready for the next club. If you ask for a favor and they say no, you think, *Fuck you, asshole! I helped you move in, cleaned your house, and painted your walls, and you won't even take me to the bloody airport because you don't want to sit in traffic?*

These are the same kinds of friends who, when they're sick, call and ask you to bring them soup. But when you're sick, they don't want to come within a mile of you because "Ew, germs!"

If you can't already tell, finding true friends in LA was not easy for me. It started when I was thirteen and it took nearly twenty years to get right, but I am now fortunate enough to have a small but solid core group of friends, and every one of us would step in front of a train to save the other.

I met my best friend in America, Dingo, when we were both still teenagers. I was struggling with not knowing very many people in a new city, when my friend Juliana said, "Look, you should meet this guy I know who also just moved here. And he's Australian!"

"That's not English!" I protested, and forgot about it until one night at Hyde. This was before clubs really started to crack down, and even if you were underage, it was easy-peasy to get in wherever you wanted. I was probably seventeen and he couldn't have been more than fifteen. He was a professional snowboarder at that time and dressed the part: neon snow pants and jacket, bandanna over his face, neon sunglasses, and a cap with the Monster energy drink logo on it. When we were introduced, I could barely even hear him speak under all his gear. *What a douche,* I thought, but then as soon as we really started chatting, we found out how much we had in common.

True, Australian and English were not the same, but we were both fish out of water as we tried to adjust to our new lives in LA (I mean, he wore a snowsuit to go out), and it was a relief to me to have some-one to hang out with who hadn't grown up in Beverly Hills and gotten a nose job to celebrate getting their high school diploma. Dingo—whose real name is Luke—and I have been friends ever since, for what now amounts to half our lives.

Though lots of people cannot believe we are not fucking or ever have, that does not mean I don't love him. I think of him as my brother. He's come along with us on family vacations. Once, while everyone else was sharing a cabin, Dingo and I found out that Mum had booked us into a romantic honeymoon suite, complete with a hot tub. Sorry, Mum, never going to happen!

In some ways, Dingo and I are the same person. We both night eat, especially if we've had a couple of drinks, and will text each other a list of what we wake up with in the bed: a jar of peanut butter, a bag of chips, a still-half-frozen frozen pizza . . .

One morning, we were on the phone, and from the spacey sound and echoes coming through on the other end, I knew he was in the bathroom.

"Are you taking a shit right now?" I asked.

"Oh God . . . ," he said. "Yes! How did you know?"

"Because I am, too!"

Still, to this day, he's the only person I've ever had a conversation with while taking a shit (and I plan to keep it that way).

Society doesn't believe in platonic friendships between men and women, but I do. Dingo is my closest, but I have so many male friends that our other friends have referred to us as Tink and her Lost Boys. I think men and women should be friends more often, because you can learn a lot from each other. Having close male friends has given me so much more respect for men and insight into the shit they go through that women never think about (like how they take things a lot more sensitively than you think they do, and all the nagging is absorbed into their heads). My guy friends can talk to me about stuff, romantic or serious, when they know their male friends would just tell them not to be a pussy about it.

Sammy and Fleur are still my two best friends in the whole world. I love my sister very much, but we couldn't be more different, and as a result, we've never been very close. Sammy and Fleur are my true sisters.

I've known Fleur since the day I was born. Her parents not only worked with my parents but are also their best friends. Her mum brought McDonald's to my mum in the hospital when I was born and laid Fleur down beside me in the crib. The way of the Osbournes was never foreign to Fleur's parents because they have been there since day one. They have always been a part of it.

I've known Sammy since my first day of nursery school. Her parents' lives, on the other hand, were a world away from my parents' lives. Her mother is a hairdresser and her father is a butcher. But not just any butcher—he is known as the best butcher for miles around. Come to think of it, maybe our fathers aren't so different after all. Both attract fans from far and wide, and both are famous for killing animals!

I spent most of my childhood Sundays at Sammy's house, where her mum would make us go on these fucking walks—"You need to get fresh air and exercise!"—where we'd be at least a begrudging ten steps behind her, in matching frog wellies,** marching through the forests and fields of the quintessential British countryside for what seemed like three hours, and then come home to a big, traditional Sunday roast.**

** TRANSLATION

🇬🇧 Wellies
🇺🇸 Rainboots

🇬🇧 Sunday roast
🇺🇸 A big family dinner that we do every Sunday

Fleur has three brothers, so whenever we were together, there was a mess of kids running and screaming around the garden. Sammy's and Fleur's parents never once treated me as if I were any different, always treating me as one of their own. They gave me some of the most "normal" experiences of my childhood and let their children step into the crazy world I lived in.

In the summers, Sammy and Fleur would come on tour with us, and they were definitely family and not guests. (I still carry a keychain with a photo of the three of us on tour.) It was usually back-to-back shows, so we'd go to sleep in one location and wake up in another. We'd shoot out of bed as soon as we heard sound check on the second stage, shower and eat as quickly as we could, then assign ourselves jobs. The three of us were little teenage blurs, unofficial production assistants sweeping floors, arranging catering, mending stage clothes, setting up my dad's quick changes, or running whatever errands needed to be run. Even with no TV on the bus, we couldn't have been bored if we'd tried.

Sammy and Fleur both still live in England, but we're as close as we've ever been. Sammy's a nurse, which was what she'd always wanted to be, ever since we were kids, and is married to Luke, who owns a very successful electrician company. They have two beautiful children. After so much exposure, Fleur fell in love with the music industry and is now a successful promoter and booking agent. We can be apart for so long, and come back together like it was just yesterday that we last saw one another. Even as I write this, I've already spoken to them both twice today.

The fact that our lives are so different now only gives us more to talk about, not less. Sammy, Fleur, and I became friends when we were young and innocent, before we'd absorbed all these ideas that friendships are about social climbing or hanging out with people who are just like you. That's why our friendship has endured: We love the true essence of one another, not the superficial stuff layered on top. I think those girls knew who I truly was before I did, and no matter what I was going through, they have always been there for me and never doubted that I am a good person.

Sammy and Fleur are truly gold, and we are all grateful that we've been able to stay friends for so long, because having a history together isn't always enough to maintain a friendship. Longevity does not automatically equal true friendship. In my late teens and early twenties, a lot of friendships were founded on being in the same place at the same time. We were all trying to figure out who the fuck we were and what we wanted out of life. Life is a journey. People move on and grow up. Everyone has their own shit to deal with.

What you have to remember is that everyone else is also on their own personal journey, so you might get to a point where suddenly you look at your relationship with someone and realize you're trying to hold on to something that's just not there anymore. Friendships fade, but the fact that it happens doesn't make it hurt less. I went through a lot of this in the past year or so with a group of friends in London.

All of a sudden, it felt like none of my calls were being returned and like I would be the only one not invited when the whole group got together. It didn't take me long to pick up the hint, even though I spent a couple of months wondering, *What the fuck did I do?* and going through my mental Rolodex to find something I had said or done to offend these people. Finally, I stopped blaming myself, and a mutual friend tipped me off to what this rift was really about: These people were jealous.

This blew my mind. Especially because jealousy is one of the most disgusting qualities a human can possess. Jealous of me? Why? To me, we were all equals. However, the more I thought about it, the more it started to make sense. I'd become friends with this group when none of us knew what the fuck we were doing with our lives. Slowly but surely, I figured my shit out, and instead of being proud of the new me and my accomplishments, they decided they liked the fat, jobless drug addict that I used to be better. That me was less intimidating and didn't remind them of all the ways they needed to sort their own lives out. I would never try to make anyone feel bad about themselves, but some people can't help but interpret someone's personal growth as a threat to their own happiness. Especially when they're not making much progress in their own lives and are still just sitting around a pub in London.

In all honesty, I did play a part in the disassembling of our relationship, because I was so busy. I couldn't keep up with the same social scene and I was less ready, willing, and able to show up anywhere, at any time, than I had been.

The friends I made during this time who I'm still close with are people who've worked as hard as they can to become successful. I met my friend Omar when he basically didn't have anyplace to live and was sleeping on couches, but since then, he has worked his ass off in fashion and marketing, and now does interior design for clients so successful that I am not even allowed to know their names. I can't even believe we're still friends, considering that the only time in his life he's ever done drugs was when I drugged him. That was probably one of the most fucked-up things I've ever done in my life. Drugs are against his religion, and it shows me how messed up I was mentally at the time that I thought it'd be funny to slip MDMA into his drink without his knowledge. Today the thought makes my skin crawl, because that's the kind of behavior that disgusts me when I look back on it. The only thing that saved our friendship after my severe lapse in judgment was that when the drugs kicked in, Omar interpreted the strange feelings he was having as a urinary tract infection. When he came down, even he thought this was so funny that he forgave me.

I am so grateful to the friends I've named here, and the dozens more who make my life as special as it is. I also try really hard to be a good friend, and remember that true friendships are equal parts give and take. I am not a big texter—I actually hate my phone—so texting me does not always get a response. I may not respond when someone texts me about a song they just heard on the radio, because I've always been this way and can't help that I'm analog. However, if one of my friends needs something, I show up. I am there for birthdays, babies, sickness, and family emergencies, and if it's what you need, I will drive you to the airport. Even in fucking Los Angeles.

*Love,*
*Kelly O*

# 12 *

# DEAR LAVENDER HAIR

You complete me. When I found you, I found myself. I am not exaggerating.

It might be hard to imagine now, because growing up I had hair like Goldilocks. It was always long, past my shoulders, and ever since I could remember, my parents were always asking me to swear on my life that I would never "fuck with it," saying that I had "hair that people would die for."

That is, until I was about thirteen and decided to take matters into my own hands.

At the time, my mum was managing the Smashing Pumpkins and had to meet the band in Ireland. She thought that this might be a nice opportunity to take Aimee and me along and let Jack and my father have some father-son time. The morning of departure, as teenage sisters do, Aimee and I got into a massive argument over something stupid, like whose T-shirt it was that was going into the suitcase.

That snowballed into an epic World War III screaming tantrum. This led my mum to realize that she could not survive the trip with the two of us there together with her. After all, this was a work trip and not a vacation. Since Aimee had been invited first, Mum decided that it was only fair that she be the one to go. Plus, my father and I always seemed to have fun no matter what state he was in, so I would be fine at home. I disagreed, however, and was so pissed off that I decided to dramatically stage one last grand protest, just in case she somehow still didn't understand how I really felt about the situation.

My bedroom in our house had a balcony that looked out over the driveway. As Mum and my sister's car was pulling out to head for the airport, I quickly ran out to the kitchen, grabbed the biggest pair of scissors I could find, and bolted back up to my bedroom and out the balcony door. As the window to the SUV rolled down, as if we were waving good-bye, I yelled, "Hey, Mum, fuck you!" (This was the first time in my life I had ever said "Fuck you" to my mum and felt like I meant it.) Then I chopped off the hair from one whole side of my head.

The gold tendrils that I'd just hacked off floated off the balcony and drifted through the air down to the first floor below, like some romantic suicide note from Rapunzel. I don't think I've ever seen my mum so shocked. She was not impressed. The car continued its course, out the driveway and to the airport, without another word being said, as the look on my mother's face said it all: I had broken her heart.

When Dad got home, he wasn't impressed, either. He took one look at me, laughed, and said, "Well, that wasn't very clever now, was it?" I shook my head because no, no it was not. He took the scissors away so I couldn't do any more damage and, as punishment, made me go to school looking like I'd gotten my hair sucked into a Flowbee.

Fortunately, he only made me go to school like that one day before he took me to the Maurice Azoulay Salon in the Beverly Hills Hotel, where Kay Lee cut it into a bob. That was the moment when I realized, *Fuck it—it's just hair. I'm not going bald anytime soon, and it will always grow back*, so I started to experiment by channeling my creativity into my hair and makeup.

After that, there were no rules when it came to hair. I cut it down to a few inches and rocked the mid-nineties Drew Barrymore platinum-bleached-spiked daisy look. Then I added black and red patches and started London spikes, followed by a Mohawk because why not? I had already gone this short. I was like Toni & Guy's wet dream. I've had Bettie Page bangs, Vargas-girl curls, and a 1960s-housewife bouffant. I've had every single hair color you could imagine, sometimes a few at the same time. The only color I wasn't allowed to do was green because if I had to stand in front of a green screen for work, I would be nothing but a floating face! I've also always stayed away from bright yellow. Yellow was always a no-go zone for me. If I dyed my hair yellow, it would be stealing from Cyndi Lauper, who I love. The album cover of hers where she has the yellow hair and red hat is absolutely legendary, and I'd never want to do anything that would even begin to infringe upon that. But pink, black, blue, red . . . all have been fair game.

To be honest, when I've had "natural" colors, the kind of shades that are supposed to look like something you could have been born with, I don't feel as much like myself as when I have a color pulled from the crayon box. When I was a brunette, I looked like my father, if he were a bloated cross-dresser or a lesbian. When I went back to blond as an adult woman, all of a sudden people I'd known my entire life—and I'm talking family friends who were practically relatives—started to hit on me. It creeped me the fuck out when men who could have changed my diapers suddenly sexualized me.

I finally landed on the shade I have now because I'm a huge Dame Edna fan and I love old ladies. To me, nothing is more punk rock than a prim little eighty-year-old with her blue-rinsed hair. When I was twelve, I snuck into my sister's room to read her fashion magazines and saw a photo in *Vanity Fair* or *Vogue*—I can't remember which—of several supermodels and one old lady, all sitting around a tea table. Each was wearing a different color suit and had her hair rinsed to match. If only I had known then how much that photo would change my life!

I loved it so much that I worked my way through all the hair colors in it, and lavender just so happened to be the last one I tried. Mixing it to find the right shade was like a chemistry experiment. I had seven different kinds of hair dye and kickers in every shade from royal purple and lavender to violet and gray. (A kicker is a final ingredient that gets added to the hair color to, as the name would imply, give a kick in one direction or another.) My colorist at the time, Judd Minter, was with me, and we mixed a new recipe in my kitchen, painted a bit on to test a strip of my hair, and then washed it out with dish soap if it wasn't right. Finally, we hit a shade that was perfect. I knew it as soon as I looked in the mirror. I didn't see purple hair—I saw the true Kelly Osbourne. I almost want to puke that I just talked about myself in the third person, but this was one of those moments.

At the time of this writing, I've had lavender hair for almost seven years, and it doesn't surprise me that I finally landed on a signature look, considering that my mum and dad are both known for their hair. Can you imagine my mum without short red hair, or my dad without his long, dark, luscious locks? I'm proud that before me and my hair, people thought that lavender hair was only for old ladies and that I started a "trend."

That said, as much as I like having a signature hair color, I haven't stopped experimenting completely. After all, our hair is such a big part of our identity and how we choose to present ourselves to the world. That is why you see girls crying in salons when they don't get the result they wanted. Hair can be very emotional!

There's a direct connection between hair and self-esteem. The expression "having a bad hair day" is a real thing—you feel like shit when your hair doesn't look good. And "good" isn't universal; rather, it's what you like and think suits you best. People often think that the fact that you are a woman means they have an open invitation to have an opinion about how you look. There will always be some cuts or colors that don't work for you because of your complexion, hair type, or the shape of your face, but never underestimate the desire of haters who will want to take down a woman—aka you—who's comfortable with how she looks and is having fun with it. This feeling isn't relegated to women only. As I get older, I am watching the emotional toll it can take on a man when he starts to see his hairline recede.

When I first dyed my hair lavender, almost everyone (including the people I worked for) were really rude about it. Comments ranged from a simple "It's ugly" to "You look like an old lady" (which, of course, I took as compliments) to "Your hair is shit and you should commit suicide." I'm not kidding—I had hundreds of thousands of comments across all my social media telling me to kill myself because of my hair color. Thank you, Internet troll twats. That's why I think it's important to have a strong sense of self and drown out every single opinion except your own when it comes to how you choose to look.

If your mum is anything like mine, and all good mothers share some universal traits, you will find that she is almost as emotionally connected to your hair as you are. Every mother has a vision of her child in an ideal form. For me, my mum's ideal version of myself was when I was somewhere around age eleven. My mum will always have a hard time when I deviate from her beautiful delusion of how she wants me to look because she wants the best for me. Mum is used to my hair color now, but she still hates it, and I can see that tiny flame of hope flickering somewhere deep inside her that burns with the desire for me to return to something a little more feminine. As I write this, I can hear her saying, "Oh, my darling Kelly, please will you change your hair?"

But for as much hate (and loving nagging) that I get about my hair, it also gets a lot of love. I get tweeted about twenty photos a day from girls who are over the moon because they've just dyed their hair and tried to do the exact same color as mine. I couldn't be happier about that. Watching people become whole after taking a leap of faith against society's standards is a beautiful thing to witness.

As serious as I am about my hair, I don't take it too seriously. The great thing about hair, like I previously stated, is that it grows back! It's not like getting a tattoo—any change you make won't have to be something you live with for the rest of your life. When it comes to ideas for new hairstyles and looks, I can find inspiration from absolutely anywhere—and I mean *anywhere*.

For example, one of my previous haircuts was a bob, shaved just on my temples. It was inspired by old photographs I'd found of nineteenth-century mental patients who'd been treated with electric shock therapy. I also found less morbid and more buttery inspiration in New York one morning, when my stylist Ryan was eating a croissant, and I decided I wanted my hair to look like a French pastry for a show I was taping that day. A quick brainstorming session, and several bobby pins and curlers later, voilà—Ryan made my wishes come true and my lavender locks had been layered and rolled into what looked like a purple croissant stuck to the back of my head. I fucking loved it.

When I went to Chris Benz's first New York Fashion Week show, I wore a yellow, orange, and pink wool dress and had my hair done in a knot of braids smack in the top center of my head because I wanted to look like a Teletubby. Take that, Jerry Falwell. I love playing with braids and once did my hair with all-over braids stuck with giant safety pins, an idea sparked by Annabella Lwin's look in the Bow Wow Wow video for "I Want Candy." I also love a good wig or throwing on some extensions when I really want to mix things up. A wig (okay, the *right* wig) instantly makes you feel mysterious and sexy, albeit incredibly hot, sweaty, and itchy. I recently wore a straight purple wig to Elton John's Oscars party, but I've also been known to wear one when going to Starbucks, or just around the house, cleaning the toilet. The point I'm trying to make is that when it comes to your hair, you don't need a reason. If you want to do it, do it.

I get that a lot of people want a gorgeous, flowy mane of golden beach waves, but that's never been me. I've tried that look before, and my reaction was always, *Why the fuck did I just pay you to do this? I could have just gotten in the ocean myself!* I've never felt like I fit in at any point of my life, and my hair is a reflection of that. I don't want to have the same hairstyle as anyone else in the room, much less *everyone* else.

My hair is one of the ways I express my individuality. You can't change who you are—and I hope you don't want to—but changing your hair can change how you feel about yourself. If you get dumped, get your hair done. If you get a new job, get your hair done. If you're depressed, get your hair done. A good stylist is practically a therapist who makes you look pretty.

So, lilac locks, thank you for everything you've done for me. I will love you forever. And don't worry—even if I have to stray for a brief time, I will always come back to you.

*Love,*
*Kelly O*

PS: Here is a list of hair tips from Frankie, who gives the most badass haircuts, and my incredible stylist Ryan.

## DON'T BE AFRAID TO TAKE RISKS.

Your hair is a direct reflection of your personality, so have fun with it. Haircuts and styles are temporary, so go ahead and push your looks to the limit—add a little strip of hidden bright color by the nape of your neck, or undercut the hair above one ear to add a little rock 'n' roll to your look. Your hair is one of the first things people notice about you, so make it something they'll remember!

## HAVING A COOL HAIRCUT IS THE ULTIMATE ACCESSORY.

If you rock a cool haircut, you can just wear jeans and a T-shirt, and you have a "look"! Confidence is the number one variable needed to pull off any look. That's why it's so important to stay true to who you are, so customize your look specifically for you.

## WHEN IT COMES TO YOUR HAIRCUT, AGE AIN'T NOTHING BUT A NUMBER.

Always go with what look will express who you are as an individual—don't let age dictate your style. If your hair doesn't reflect who you are, your clothes and makeup won't have the same impact!

## WHEN IN DOUBT, GO WITH PERFECTLY IMPERFECT.

The chicest hair is undone hair. If your hair looks like you've spent days in the chair, you've done too much.

## NEVER UNDERESTIMATE THE POWER OF A PONY!

From day to night, beach to Broadway, a ponytail is always appropriate. Play with texture and placement . . . there's a ponytail for every statement you want to make!

## GET YOUR GEAR RIGHT.

#Protip: Invest in quality appliances. Yes, they are more money up front, but your hair (and pocketbook!) will thank you long term. You won't have to replace them, and they'll be more effective and gentler on your tresses. Product formulation has come a long way, so do your research and get the right stuff for you. At-home conditioners, especially for those of you with fantasy colors of hair, can maintain your vibrant or pastel hues without weekly visits to salons. Ryan is never without his L'Oréal Elnett hair spray, Oribe Dry Texturizing Spray, and a Mason Pearson brush.

# 13 *

......................................................................

# DEAR FASHION

You are one of my greatest loves. Music is a passion embedded in my DNA. Fashion is the passion that I *chose*, and for me, the two influences are nearly inextricable. From the time I was a little girl, I always loved dressing up. When we lived in the country village I grew up in, all my clothes came from a place called Wendy House. It was the only children's clothing store for miles. When their new shipment came in, all the mums got super competitive and would fight trying to get their daughter the prettiest party dress in the village. If you think "dance moms" are bad, you should meet the "village mums."

While Mum did most of my clothes shopping, Dad often bought things that he liked and that he assumed I would like, too. Let's just say that whatever he bought me was always interesting.

One specific time, I remember he had just come back from tour, and I was getting ready to go to a friend's birthday. When I was a little girl, most people still dressed little girls like little girls—not like today, when people are dressing toddlers in fashion-forward, trendy clothing. We had to wear dresses when we were getting dressed up, and they were always very frilly, floral affairs.

I had mine on, all ready to go, but Dad took one look at me and said, "What, you're not going to wear the dress that I brought you?"

Mum sensed that his feelings were hurt and said, "Kelly, put that dress on."

Now, I really did love that dress—I just loved it so much that I thought I would save it for a really special occasion, not just another birthday at the Beaconsfield Village Hall.

However, I didn't want to risk Dad thinking that I didn't like it, so I went back to my room to change my dress. When I came out to show it off, Mum could barely keep a straight face. Dad thought I looked brilliant, and so off I went in a Carmen Miranda costume, complete with long ruffled skirt, off-the-shoulder top, and a headband covered in fake fucking fruit.

My friends' parents still bring it up to this day. "Remember when you were six years old and came dressed as . . ."

Yes. Yes, I remember.

Mum was always very good about letting me pick out what I wanted to wear. One of my prized possessions was a nylon T-shirt covered with a bright yellow taxi print. It was made from this cheap fabric that is often also used to make Halloween costumes. I thought I was so cool, completely unaware that I was also highly flammable. If anyone had come near me with a lighter, I would have exploded.

When we moved to America, I started to shop more for myself. Not because the shopping was any better (American versus British fashion: that's a whole other topic) but because I was thirteen and finally old enough to go out on my own. I would go shopping at Fred Segal and Target, and yes, a confession, Hot Topic, where I would buy those sock-fabric sweatband bracelets in every single color.

One of our favorite haunts was the Century City Mall, where Mum would drop me off to meet my friends to hang out for the night. She'd be back at ten on the dot to pick us up in the exact same spot, and we were always right on time, knowing that we'd be in trouble if we were more than three minutes late.

Coming from England, where teenagers would spend most of their social time gathering around a park bench, the mall seemed like a wonderland to my brother and me. This was before everyone had cell phones, so since we couldn't call or text anyone, we'd hang out in front of the movie theater, the unofficial meeting spot, to see if anyone else was going to show up.

At this point, I was starting to get interested in the idea of fashion, beyond just what T-shirt I put on, and magazines were my primary source of information, so I spent most of my pocket money, and time, at the bookshop. I could spend hours browsing the editorials, seeing how outfits were put together, and reading the credits so I could learn about different designers.

It was at this formative time in my life, as I came into adolescence, that I discovered punk like the Sex Pistols, Iggy Pop, and X-Ray Spex, and I loved Boy George and Haysi Fantayzee. (Don't get me wrong, these musicians did not steal any spotlight from my beloved boy bands; it is just that these influences had a greater influence on how I viewed style.) Later on, I would become obsessed with the Strokes, which turned me on to artists like Lou Reed and the Velvet Underground.

At this time, given how my mind worked, and knowing that all these people didn't just wake up one day and decide to start dressing like that, I dug in and did my research. I learned about Zandra Rhodes, and how she was the first person to put safety pins on the runway, and how Vivienne Westwood and Malcolm McLaren spawned an entire fashion movement with their store SEX. This led me further down the fashion path to Blitz Kids** and the New Romantics.

**★★ TRANSLATION**

Blitz Kids

Kids who frequented the Blitz night in Covent Garden in the late '70s and early '80s and launched the New Romantics cultural movement

I soaked it all up, but my interest was very much at a distance and almost academic—I didn't think that fashion was something I could participate in. I reasoned that I didn't look like a supermodel, so I couldn't wear any of the clothes. I was a total teenage tomboy. I wore a wallet chain and carried a skateboard that, if anyone asked about, I would say I was just holding for a friend.

I wore a sports bra every single day, even if my only sport was watching telly, because my weight fluctuated so much that I felt as if my breasts were a different size every time I woke up. I could be an A cup on Saturday and a DD on Monday. I was constantly embarrassed, because I was sure that everyone else noticed as much as I did.

In England, Mum took me to a special shop where the Queen and other members of the Royal Family bought their bras, the kind of shop where a posh lady comes into the dressing room with you, puts her cold hands and a measuring tape all over your boobs, and tells you you're wearing the wrong size. When she finished and came back holding a FF that looked like you could fit a pumpkin into each cup, I burst into tears.

*Fuck this,* I thought. *I hate my tits.* I slept on my stomach every night, hoping to flatten out my breasts. You couldn't have paid me to wear a dress, or anything tighter than a T-shirt. I loved fashion, but I wore clothes.

The first time I ever worked with a stylist was when I signed a record deal and had to do press photos for the label. I was only fifteen, so my parents had strict rules for me. I couldn't show my cleavage or be too sexy, but I also give Mum and Dad a lot of credit. They were very adamant that I look like myself, and they wouldn't let the label turn me into what they thought was the look of a sanitized, contrived, caricaturized teenybopper star. I resisted any attempt anyone made to push me in that direction. I was sure as hell not going to be punk with an X. If I was going to be punk-anything, it was real punk.

By the grace of God, the label had hired Brooke Dulien to style the shoot. Brooke had a jewelry line and store called White Trash Charms that sold all kinds of stuff handmade by LA designers, from Brooke's gold lightning bolt and mud flap girl necklaces to reworked vintage by Deathcamp (a group of struggling artists who all lived in one chaotic house where someone's "room" was a mattress shoved up against the wall on the landing of a staircase) to custom screen prints from Uniform Circa.

From the moment Brooke and I met, it was obvious that we were sisters from different misters. I still remember what I was wearing that day: a red-and-white-striped shirt, blue jeans, red leather Converse that had elastic instead of laces, and a green Marc Jacobs jacket. Brooke told me she had the same jacket. She was wearing a B earring. I was wearing a K earring. It was love.

In the pre-Internet era, the only way to see fashion editorials was to buy magazines, and I bought them by the dozen. Prior to the shoot,

I spent hours compiling tear sheets of the looks and references that I liked. Brooke had pulled some of the exact same ones, and she looked at me and said, "Kelly, besides Gwen Stefani, you are the only person out of my entire client roster who has ever shown up with a vision of what they wanted to look like."

She told me that the looks I pulled were exactly what she'd imagined for me and that I reminded her so much of Gwen. "I swear to God, Kelly," she said, "one day you're going to have a fashion line." That day I didn't believe her, but Brooke knew best.

Even as a teenager, I knew that fashion is all about reinvention. In every look, in every outfit, there has to be one thing that diverges from the expected. This is what makes people think and makes fashion creative, but it's a line that's easy to cross, which is why you see so many people who try to follow so many "trends" that it looks like fashion threw up on them.

Brooke and I envisioned the shoot as if John Galliano were our creative director. We'd rework and revamp pieces so that everything was a little off. If something was pretty, we'd tweak it so it had a punk edge, and vice versa.

The whole shoot was guerrilla-style, with no permits. We were running up and down Hollywood Boulevard with armloads of jackets and skirts, and I was changing in the bathroom at McDonald's. Since I was so young, and Mum was still my manager, she had to approve every outfit and setup before we shot it. Brooke would take Polaroids and then dispatch a runner to Mum's office to show her and get her okay. We shot on the Walk of Fame, right next to my dad's star, in my garden with an umbrella, and finally outside my house, with me standing on the roof of a Mini Cooper.

Before that shoot, I hadn't ever thought that fashion was something for me. I just thought I was an observer on the outside looking in, but this was one of the first times I'd ever felt good about myself and how I looked in clothes. It was one of the most incredible days of my life, and from then on, Brooke was my partner in fashion crime. It was the beginning of a personal and professional relationship that has lasted more than fifteen years. Brooke gave me my first pair of high heels, pink Versace pumps, and I still have them.

At the time, irony wasn't popular, but everything Brooke and I did was all about taking the piss out of clothing. We commissioned Deathcamp and Uniform Circa to make custom pieces for my shoots. We covered everything with pins and patches and took articles of clothing that everyone else hated, and turned them into something that we loved, like a Members Only jacket made punk with safety pins.

Soon, I was able to read a briefing for a shoot and know immediately whether I was going to hate it; I didn't have to even see the clothes. I'd play along and put the dress on, then stand there as everyone took in the fact that I looked like a pregnant teen who'd just been tarred and feathered.

I was never a brat about it, because this is how the game is played and I am always game to play it. Everyone has their own artistic vision for what works in a particular look, and it is important to listen and try each idea—because you never know! I'm not going to lie, though— nine times out of ten, it was like the Big Bird routine above, and we would end up going with my initial instinct.

When Brooke and I were collaborating on the look for my "One Word" video, I was at a time in my life when I was ready to step away from punk and move on. I had spent hours watching French New Wave films and had become enamored of Anna Karina's tragic, glamorous look. It was only a year or two prior that I'd have thrown a fit if anyone tried to pry me out of my jeans and Converse; now I wore a sleek long black wig, fitted waists, and high heels. To me, New Wave was an evolution of angst—the teenage frustration transforming into passion, but with no less disillusionment—and "One Word" is still my favorite video I ever made.

Brooke was more than just my stylist. She was my therapist and hand-holder through every big fashion transition I had to make, and since these usually were the result of major life transitions as well, she got me through a lot. Becoming more comfortable playing around with how I looked didn't necessarily translate into being comfortable with how I looked. If Brooke took Polaroids before I'd had my hair and makeup done, I'd make her scratch out my face so I wouldn't have to look at it. That was how insecure I was at the time.

I'd always hidden behind my hair and makeup, sometimes with a swath of bangs sweeping across my face and covering my eyes, but Brooke was the one to convince me that it was time to grow up for red carpets. The idea of wearing less makeup scared the fuck out of me, because even when I'd gone for what I considered a natural look before, it was still a shitload of makeup. Now I kept my hair and makeup simple and wore fancy evening gowns. I showed off not only my face but my figure as well, and for the first time showed people what I really looked like. People were shocked, and it was the first time in my life that the media had called me beautiful. Then I was the one who was shocked.

I trusted Brooke, and a few years later, when I went to my first

New York Fashion Week, she picked every single item I wore. I'd been to a few fashion shows here and there before, but this time I went to make a statement. I'd always been serious about fashion, but I'd never really shown that to the world, and now I was ready.

The first look Brooke had picked was for Gwen Stefani's L.A.M.B. presentation at Milk Studios. It was a terrifying little minidress that glittered, with structured shoulder pads. It was short and tight as fuck. I took one look at it and said, "I can't wear this dress!"

*Short* and *tight* still weren't in my fashion vocabulary at that point, and my only previous minidress experience was a bad one. Shortly after I'd lost all the weight, I did a photo shoot for a magazine that shall not be named. They made me squeeze into a tube dress, and even though I looked banging in it, it wasn't me. Rather than chic, I looked cheap and felt really uncomfortable. When I told them I wasn't ready to dress like that, the woman running the shoot was a first-rate mean girl, and she was so mean about it that I started to cry. Now what had started out as mild trepidation turned into a full-blown tight-dress phobia.

But with Brooke's help, I sucked up all the confidence I could muster and put that LBD on. The minute I walked into the L.A.M.B. presentation, everyone gasped. I panicked and ran to the bathroom. Brooke came running after me, asking what was wrong.

"Everyone is gasping. I knew I shouldn't have worn this dress."

"Kelly, everyone *is* gasping. But not out of disgust. They are gasping because you took their breath away. You look gorgeous."

In that moment, I knew it was worth it and I also realized the magnitude of the insecurity that it was time to get over. I pulled myself together and we walked back into the room. Gwen stopped mid-conversation to come over and say hello to me, with every paparazzo furiously snapping photos.

It was the LBD that changed my life. The next day, three hundred dresses showed up at our hotel. Every designer wanted to dress me. Brooke and I couldn't believe it. We'd accept one delivery, scream and dance around when we saw the clothes inside, and then just as soon as we'd calmed down from that one, the door would buzz and it would start all over again. We raced around like chickens with our heads cut off that whole week, running back to my now trashed hotel room that was covered wall to wall with breathtaking clothing to change so that I could wear each designer's clothes to their show, and never make the fashion faux pas of wearing the same thing twice.

That whole week, I was Brooke's doll, and I learned the true value of a stylist.

A good stylist can make you look like anyone.

A great stylist elevates you while still making you look like yourself.

When Brooke told me to try something new that I never thought I'd be able to pull off, I learned to swallow my insecurities and try it anyway. Brooke never failed me. She was so in tune with my taste and style that she instinctively knew what would look good on me and make heads turn. That week changed my life and secured me a spot as a participant in a world I'd always loved but had theretofore believed I could only admire from a distance.

Now when I'm asked about fashion, nine times out of ten it's because someone expects me to give them a guide to looking cool, and I can't do that. I'm not going to be able to tell you how to change your life with a dress. What makes you cool is not what you wear but the confidence with which you wear it. You can wear a garbage bag and look incredible if you're confident enough to pull it off.

I really have only two rules when it comes to fashion. One: Use your imagination. Two: Leave something to the imagination (also known as the "No one wants to see your klacker" rule).

From the Blitz Kids, I learned that you can turn anything in your house into something you can wear. My dad was doing this decades before the Blitz Kids. The first time he met my mum, he'd made himself a necklace out of a tap tied onto a shoestring and paired it with striped pajamas. Needless to say, he scared Mum to death (though obviously, she got over it).

Recently, I was about to go on set at *Australia's Got Talent*, and I felt my hair was lacking something. After digging through my stylist's kit, I found a broken gold chain necklace that I wrapped around the top of my bun. It transformed and completed the whole look. I guess it's true what they say: One woman's trash is another woman's treasure.

Fashion isn't about what you wear but how you wear it. For example, when Mum gave me an Hermès Birkin bag, I didn't feel like it was me and I never carried it. When she inquired about it, I explained that to me, the bag was simply a status symbol—not a fashion symbol. The bag had lost its luxurious value because I was seeing it everywhere. Mum asked if I wanted something else, and when I declined, she returned with the same bag, but this time it had patches sewn all over it. One of them read "Amateur Gynecologist." And just like that, the handbag had been transformed from something totally overdone to something entirely unique and special. Something that felt like me.

I realize that to some, the bag was ruined. But to many others and, most important, to myself, it was perfection.

When it comes to fashion, you have to make things your own. Like I said before, it's all about that twist, that tiny bit of reinvention that makes something unique. I love shopping at high-street stores** because the clothes are a blank canvas I can transform into something new—either with the change of a button or tailoring the length of the hem. I know celebrities who will cut labels like these out and replace them with designer labels like Prada or Alexander McQueen. I was once with a high-profile person (who shall remain nameless) who freaked out when she lost her jacket at Beacher's Madhouse. I helped her look all over for it, thinking it must be really expensive for her to be so worried. But no, not at all—turns out it was from Zara, and she just didn't want anyone to know. I laughed my ass off and stopped helping her look.

** TRANSLATION

High-street stores

The high street is the main street in your town, where all the shops, banks, and businesses are. High-street stores are often big-name, fast-fashion retailers.

I've been everything from a size 0 to a size 14, and I know that labels, styles, and trends mean shit. You only have to pay attention to and wear what looks good on you, and what fits. For example, it's a rare breed of woman who is able to pull off an empire-waist maxi dress, so the rest of us should leave them to her, even if it seems like they're everywhere this season. Tailoring can also be your best friend, especially if you're short like me, because no matter who's on the label or what's on the price tag, an article of clothing won't look chic on you if it's too long, too short, too tight, or too big.

After years of being insecure about my body, I have stashed a few tricks up my tailored sleeve. I know to throw on a shoulder pad when I want my waist to look smaller, or to wear a long shirt when I'm worried about my thigh gap (or more specifically, my lack thereof). I've learned about the magic of draping and that there are wonderful things you can do with a few layers.

But I still think the most important aspect of how to dress well is to just have some fucking fun. Wear things that make you laugh or smile, and skip clothing that makes it so you can't breathe or eat or dance. Try something new. Change it up. Evolve. Surprise everyone. Surprise yourself. Write your own fashion rules instead of subscribing to someone else's. Yes, even mine.

*Love,*
*Kelly O*

PS: Here are a few style and fashion tips from Brooke Dulien, my eternal partner in fashion crimes and misdemeanors.

## TAKE A PICTURE, IT'LL LAST LONGER!

Take a photo of your look from the front and the back. This will help you make sure you picked the right underwear and don't have any panty line or bra mishaps. It will also help you make sure nothing is too (unintentionally) sheer in the daylight and that it's flattering from all angles. You can also play with different accessories and compare them side by side.

## STAINS ARE NOT SEXY.

Pack a stain remover pen in your purse. Tide and OxiClean have amazing ones that are no bigger than your average writing pen, and they can help save an outfit from too much fun.

## DON'T FORGET YOUR LBJ (LITTLE BLACK JACKET).

The little black dress is definitely an important piece in every girl's wardrobe, but you should make your little black jacket just as important. You can dress it up with heels and a dress, or dress it down with jeans and flats. You can always just throw your LBJ over your shoulders instead of wearing it traditionally. Kelly always makes her look unique and often embellishes her jacket with cool vintage brooches or pins from high-street shops like H&M and Topshop. She always dresses it differently from how it was sold, which is why she's such a fashion icon and so many girls want to emulate her look!

## JUST THE TIPS.

Don't forget your manicure and pedicure—they're the key to polishing any look! Streamline with a French manicure, or raise your fashion bar with cool-girl multicolored gels.

## TAILOR EVERYTHING TO YOUR NEEDS.

Don't be intimidated by the word *tailor*. Your local cleaners usually has an in-house tailor who is absolutely affordable. Kelly knows her body and always knows when to take a hem up or down—plus, knowing your clothes fit perfectly gives you that much more confidence in your look!

# 14 *

......................................................................................

# DEAR VAGINA

## *WARNING: IF YOU ARE IN MY FAMILY, YOU MIGHT WANT TO SKIP THIS CHAPTER!

Being a woman is complicated. The addition of a Y chromosome means our brains work differently from men's, and we have to go through all kinds of stuff with our bodies that men will just never understand.

For instance: you, vagina. You are a very complex body part, and we don't need science to tell us that most men don't know a damn thing about you.

My true belief is that porn has ruined the state of affairs for vaginas the world over. Forget mystique—everyone has seen it all, but without the much-needed disclaimer that most of the vaginas in porn are man-made. Guys who watch a lot of porn now think they're going to get a cute little quarter-slot vagina, and it's not like that. Vaginas are like fingerprints—they're all unique and come in all shapes and sizes. I hate that they've also now become yet another body part that causes women to feel as though they don't measure up to some porn star who's got a whole bag of tricks up her . . . hood?

Another way I think porn has warped views on sex is that it makes people think that all women like the same things. That's not true at all. I have never particularly liked cunnilingus, even though porn and movies would make you think that going down on a woman makes her want to marry you.

For me, though, it's always been an intensely uncomfortable experience. All I do is lie there, staring at the ceiling and thinking, *Oh my God, what if it smells? It's so ugly. His face is right near my butthole. What if I fart? I'm not enjoying this. I'm getting a sweaty top lip; not on my vagina, but my face. I really want this to stop. He keeps asking me if it feels good and he's poking my vagina while he's sticking his tongue in there. I really can't do this. How much longer am I going to have to pretend this is enjoyable? It feels like he's spitting on me.*

When I'm dating someone new, it doesn't take long for me to let him know that's a no-go zone for me. Most guys are kind of disappointed by this, but I've learned that as the owner of a vagina, it's important to have open conversations about how you want it to be treated and operated. This prevents some weird, and often quite shocking, discoveries along the way.

Popular feminist wisdom will tell that you're supposed to be real proud of your klacker, but I reserve the right to feel however I want to feel about mine. I'm not insecure about my vagina; I'm just realistic. Vaginas birth life, and that's beautiful, but I've taken the mirror out and had a good old look—and it's still ugly. I have great respect for it, but do I want to show it off? Hell. No.

I plan to be like Joan Rivers and never retire, but I do have one rule about ending my career: If the world ever sees my vagina, I am out. I will quit and go back to England and become the farm girl I have always secretly wanted to be. I'll slowly fade from people's memories, except for every once in a while, when someone brings up my name: "Whatever happened to Kelly?"

"Oh, you know, we all saw her vagina, so she left."

I will never understand people who go out without knickers,** knowing that there are paparazzi just standing at the curb, waiting for them to accidentally (or maybe on purpose?) spread their knees as they get out of the car. Nope, that is not for me. Life in the public eye has to come with some limits, and for me, my body is one of them. Whenever there's a major phone-hacking scandal and celebrities' nudes get leaked, there's always someone who's gotten the camera right up in there to snap some photos. I'm all about celebrating your body, but I've never stuck the selfie lens down between my legs and taken a photo of my beef curtains, thinking, *Mmm-hmm, that's so hot, better take a photo and text it.*

**\*\* TRANSLATION**

🇬🇧 Knickers

🇺🇸 Underwear. Do not say "panties"—I fucking hate that word!

Recently, I was hanging out with my friend Shaun Ross, who's a well-known male model, and I was wearing one of my favorite articles of clothing—sweatpants. I'd rolled the waist several times to shorten them up and they became tighter around my crotch.

Shaun took one look at me and goes, "Mmmm, girl, you got that puffy puss, too, and you're still single?"

My reaction? I freaked out. "Uh, what's *puffy puss*? Does that mean I have a fat vagina, too?"

Shaun started laughing and told me all about it. Puffy puss was something some guys are now into—they think it's hot—and so that's why girls pull their jeans up really high and into the groin. I had no idea that our society is now at a point where I am supposed to make my vagina look appealing even with clothes on, but you learn something new about being a woman every day, and usually it's terrifying.

Shortly after I dyed my hair lavender, Joan asked me if the carpet matched the drapes, and I told her there was no carpet. She tried to convince me that pubic hair was there for a reason—to provide friction—but I'm not having it. I am not a fan of pubic hair, and in my case, I think the barer down there, the better.

This does not mean I'm a fan of getting waxed.

Oh no, quite the opposite.

It is an experience I absolutely hate.

I'm never in one place long enough to build up a rapport with any one aesthetician in particular, and I don't like anyone blowing on my vagina, especially a stranger. I remember the first time that happened, I was shocked. There I am in a tiny room, spread-eagled on a table, and some woman I just met five minutes ago smears hot wax across my pubes, then leans over and starts blowing on it to cool it off. I was so freaked out that I never told anybody; then I saw an interview with Rihanna where she was talking about it. I thought, *Oh my God, they do that to her, too?!* After that, I knew I was staying away, because there are secret blowers all over the place.

I have been known to call my vagina the Revenant when it gets especially hairy, but since I believe in good grooming, I take de-hairing into my own hands. If I'm just around my house, smelly and sweaty is no big deal, but there is no way that I am stepping into the outside world until I've brushed my teeth, showered, shaved what little is left, and put clean clothes on.

That's basic shit, but there's a new trend with some girls where they're not showering every day—or even more than two days!—and it's gross. Proper hygiene is not bourgeois, and having a smelly vagina does not make you a rebel. I'm not saying that everyone go out and buy Vaggie Wipes, but soap, water, and a razor should be a part of every vagina's daily maintenance routine.

There's also medical maintenance, too. When I was a teenager, my sister took it upon herself to book me a gynecologist appointment. This was probably because everyone thought I was doing shit that I wasn't—like having sex. Little did they know, I was a prude.

Everything went to shit when the office called to confirm the appointment and I answered on speaker phone while in the car with my mum. This was all captured in an episode of *The Osbournes*, and I was completely embarrassed. I was really shy and hated the fact that other people were even talking about what I had going on between my legs. I freaked out and immediately canceled. I couldn't see the point in going if no one had ever even touched it.

When I turned eighteen, I finally went for my first appointment. Like with every visit to the gyno, they made me put on that stupid paper gown and sheet. When the doctor came in and told me to put my feet in the stirrups, I burst into tears. "I don't want anyone to see my vagina!" I blubbered.

The doctor took one look at me and said, "Oh, shut up. You think I've never seen a vagina before? We get one of you a week. I'll be back in five minutes." She was so matter-of-fact and unaffected by the whole thing that I did exactly what she said and didn't even start crying again when she inserted a duck-looking piece of metal into me and started clunking it around like a mechanic changing a tire.

Being a woman also seems to involve a lot of bewildering underwear, even though I managed to make it to age thirty without wearing a thong.

Okay, wait, that's not entirely true.

When I was in ninth grade, I really wanted day-of-the-week underwear. Mum accidentally bought me a package of thongs, instead of the full-butt kind. I don't think she even realized it, so I wore them anyway.

One day after school, I came home and dropped my backpack on the floor. When I bent over to start rifling through it, Dad saw my whale-tail creeping up above my jeans and flipped out. "No daughter of mine is going to wear a throng!" he screamed. Yes, he called it a "throng," and then he proceeded to cut said throng off me with a pair of scissors. Needless to say, after that, I had a full-blown thong phobia.

I also just didn't want to wear underwear that went up my ass and made me feel like I had an eternal wedgie, so I went with granny panties for all occasions. One day, a stylist I was working with came to a meeting with a bunch of printed-out pictures of me on the red carpet. "Look," she said, pointing at my ass.

I immediately realized what people meant when they said "visible panty line." I looked like I had Picasso arse—the lines of my knickers multiplying my two cheeks into four.

"Okay," I agreed, "I'll wear a thong. I promise."

"Don't worry," she assured me. "Once your butthole gets callused and scarred, you won't even feel it."

*Fucking hell*, I thought, *this is going to be even worse than I'd imagined!*

I was determined, though. If every other woman out there on the red carpet could wear one, then so could I. Plus, I'd promised, and I hate to break a promise.

The stylist forced me to wear a thong for an entire month—the whole time with me waiting for my asshole to toughen up—before she finally copped to the joke. "I still can't believe you fell for that callused butthole act!" she said. Well, how the fuck was I supposed to know?! I was too scared to Google it!

After learning how to wear a thong—and let's be honest, there really isn't much learning; you just put up with having a string up your ass—I have since been enlightened to yet another undignified female undergarment: Spanx. Spanx suck the FUPA in, for which I am very grateful, but they are disgusting. I am a human hot water bottle—my mum says that when I go through menopause, my family will have to scatter and pretend they've never met me before in their lives—and within five minutes of putting on Spanx, I start to sweat.

As I'm walking around with all my fat mashed into my organs, I can just picture the layer of sweat gathering between me and the Spanx and about how it's all going to smell like pissy plastic down there. And just when you thought female undergarments couldn't get any more undignified.

Yes, they're a lot of work, but if you do have a vagina, you should consider yourself lucky! Women have always known that a vagina means power, but now we are fortunate enough to be living in a time that finally acknowledges this. Everywhere you look, vaginas are on top, which is just one more reason to treat yours with the respect it deserves.

*Love,*
*Kelly O*

# 15 *

........................................................................................

# DEAR DATING

You and I have never quite seen eye to eye. I'm a romantic person at heart, but when someone has been shit on as many times as I have, it's hard to let the right people in.

Dating used to be a pretty civilized affair, but I think the Internet has blown that all to hell. It used to be that one person would ask another person out on a date, and then they'd gradually get to know each other. Now, thanks to social media and text messaging, flirting is a series of likes, pokes, and lurking (aka stalking). The result is that you can feel as though you know *everything* about someone you may never have laid eyes on in real life, much less properly met.

You can write someone off for the stupidest thing (for me, that used to be Radiohead fans who used the word *existential* too much) or allow yourself to make all kinds of assumptions based on a few photos (maybe that young girl dancing sexy on a pole has never even seen a penis in her whole life).

Here is a piece of advice: With the amount of info that is out there about every single person, you have to exercise some self-control. Do not go on Facebook and look at his or her ex and then obsess about it. Someone's past is their past—we all have one—and chances are, if you do enough digging, you're going to end up finding out something you didn't want to know. Once you know something, you can't un-know it.

It's almost impossible to have an honest relationship with someone when you know a lot more about that person than you're letting on. You will just be paranoid and become obsessed, especially if you can't stop thinking about some anonymous ex from the past. The fact is, they are not dating that anonymous person from the past. They are dating you. Case closed.

As someone who has been labeled so many different things in my life, I have had to work really fucking hard to get where I am now. I want people to judge me as the person I am today when they meet me, not as the person I was ten or fifteen years ago or even yesterday. My past is shoved in my face daily. I know it's really hard, but it is important to live in the moment with people. Dating someone for who they used to be, or who you think they're going to be in the future, isn't fair and is just going to frustrate you both.

People could save themselves a lot of trouble if they just realized a couple of things: boys are stupid and girls are cunts. It's really not that hard to please a girl. Just be straight with her. If you're going out with your mates and you know it's going to be a late one, just tell her you don't know what time you'll be back, so don't wait up. Don't lie and say, "Uh, I'll be back at nine," and then not answer the phone when she calls at ten because she's worried that you got run over by a train. When she freaks out over something like this, it's not because she's "crazy"—it's because you went and made a really simple situation complicated.

Girls, don't be so manipulative. People can't read minds, so just say what you're thinking and save both of you the trouble. Don't waste your time coming up with some elaborate scheme to try to trick someone into doing what you want and then get pissed when they are oblivious to the hints you're dropping—subtle or not. Men are not nuanced creatures. They will trip over a hint before they ever pick up on it.

For any relationship to truly work, you have to be honest with yourself and with each other. If your boo doesn't want you to have the password to his phone, there's probably a reason. If you do have the password to his phone, then it's because he has nothing to hide and trusts you, so don't go scrolling through his texts until you find something from eight months ago that you can get pissed about. It's a little thing called dignity. I know it's not very common anymore, but let's all try to bring a little of it back.

I don't online date, but I'm glad my friends do, because it's hilarious! They get so many dick pics, and these guys do this without being asked! They're just convinced that we all can't wait to see their cocks, when in reality, most of the time we're showing all our friends, laughing our asses off, and thinking, *Put that thing away.* One time a friend of mine got sent a dick pic that we swear was taken with a selfie stick! So much preparation for something so embarrassing.

The first time I ever got sent a dick pic, I didn't even ask for it. It just popped up on my phone at three thirty in the afternoon. I was in a big huge conference room filled with agents from William Morris. This was during the time when Apple was advertising brighter screens and bigger phones, and I looked down and thought, *What the fuck?* It was from a guy I didn't even know liked me, and I had to read our text exchange three times over before I finally understood that he had misconstrued our conversation as me flirting. How did he think I was going to respond? "Oh, thank you! That dick pic really got me through that three thirty feeling!"

This was one of those instances where I told myself, *Okay, I don't understand men and I never will.* Do they not think we know that this is the same dick pic they've sent to twenty-four other women and shot at least twenty-five angles of to make it look bigger? Just like a fart, penises will always be funny.

I think everyone can agree that whether you're gay, straight, whatever, the worst part about dating is finding the right person. It's hard for me to find someone I can tolerate for even five minutes, much less twenty-four hours or my entire life. One day, my friend Jen and I were leaving her apartment and passed her Greek landlady, who filled the pool every day with a red hose, even when we were in the middle of one of California's biggest droughts. As we passed, she called out and told us we looked beautiful and to have a beautiful day, then reminded us to "remember it's LA. Evvvvvvvvvverybody piece of shit!"

Just before we got to the gate, she asked Jen, "You have boyfriend yet?"

When Jen said no, the landlady said, "You wait, I have present for you. It's gonna help." She then turned around and disappeared into her apartment.

Jen and I looked at each other in anticipation, wondering what the fuck she was going to bring out that would help us get boyfriends. Padded underwear? A magic spell? Funky Cold Medina?**

**\*\* TRANSLATION**

Funky Cold Medina
From the Tone Loc song, like a love potion

It was a handbag. Specifically, it was quite the ugliest handbag ever known to man. Made of vinyl and fake tortoise shell, lined in paisley, adorned with rhinestones and gold-toned hardware, emblazoned with the word *Paparazzi* down the side. "Here, this will help you," the landlady said, handing it over.

Jen was clearly shocked. "Oh, I don't know what to say," she said as she accepted it. "Thank you?"

If I didn't feel like a spinster before, I definitely felt like one in that moment.

Once we left, we discovered a QR code printed on the bottom of the actual bag as part of the design! We scanned it, and the link took you to buy a printer on Amazon.com. Well, Jen and I carried that hideous bag around Los Angeles for an entire day, but still no boyfriends.

Even when you find the right person, relationships are still work. It's not just fantasy. You can't just expect glittery romance and rose petals all the time. People tend to think that being in a relationship means never feeling lonely, always being happy, and having someone there to fulfill all their needs, whether that means going to the bar to get them a drink or listening to them bitch about their day for two hours every night after they get home from work.

People are thinking so much about what they can get out of a relationship that they never think about what they need to put into the relationship. It amazes me that people are then shocked when it doesn't work out. One of my dating rules is to do one nice thing a day for the person I'm with, because they need to feel special, too. It does not have to be grandiose, just something as simple as doing the dishes or running a nice, hot bath.

Another one of my rules is, if the relationship isn't working for you, end it clean and quick. Don't dither about, thinking, *I feel so bad; if I break up with him, he'll be devastated*, because (a) he probably won't be, and (b) even if he is, at least you stopped wasting everyone's time. I'm so guilty of breaking my own rule on this, but after a few messy experiences, I've learned that you have to end it when it's time. There's no kindness in stringing someone along.

Even though I was lost and unhappy and lonely for much of my life, I still think I had a solid understanding of love. I couldn't always stop myself from being infatuated with boys. I was still aware of the fine line between love and obsession from an early age.

This is evidenced by my 2001 journal, or my "girlnal," as I call it. In it, I had written so many poems. Here's an example of how deep I so clearly was:

> As the morning grey sets on another day of cold frosty
>    obsession,
> I still search for what I strive to be. Fear of telling and
>    hearing an ear piercing reply.
> Tears falling off the round, pillowy cheeks of my face.
> There is no reason for it all, but the front door to my life
>    is locked and bolted. Maybe the search for the key will
>    kill me.

*Maybe it lies in my fist-sized heart, which beats for my
obsession.*

I mean . . . in 2001 I was a baby! I didn't even have a driver's license yet, but no one could ever accuse me of not being deep as a puddle. I am willing to bet my life I wrote this while listening to Depeche Mode or the Cure after putting on a ton of black eyeliner, as if the more I put on, the more profound I was proving myself to be.

My first real boyfriend dumped me over the phone, and on Valentine's Day. He was the first boy who ever broke my heart. It was the pain of losing my innocence.

The cuts from a first love go deep, and some of my friends still aren't over theirs, even though they've had twenty years and two husbands to do it. That first heartbreak is enough to make you crazy and is debilitating in so many ways, but am I glad I got to have that experience? Yes. Absolutely. First love is special, but when I look back, this is one of those experiences that meant so much to me at the time but means practically nothing now. I don't know if that is maturity or cynicism. Most likely, it is a combination of both.

Women always know when men are lying to them; it's just that sometimes we choose not to believe it. For almost two years, I was dating a musician. One morning, the guy rolled over and, while looking deep into my eyes, said, "I love you. Tell me you love me and I'll never leave you."

This was the first time a guy had ever told me he loved me first. So naturally, I believed him and confessed that I was in love with him, too. It was mere days later when I found out that he'd had a fiancée the whole time. That broke my heart and messed with my head.

Amy Winehouse was living with me at the time. As one of my

closest friends, she was one of the few people I talked to about it. She taught me so much about love. When it came to giving other people advice on matters of the heart, she was one of the smartest people I've ever known.

"Kelly Bollocks," she said, because she always called me Kelly Bollocks, or Lul, which was what she called her closest friends, "I know this is breaking your heart, but you need to understand that what you had with him, no one can take away, and what you had with him, he will never have with anyone else again. Your feelings were real. I know you loved him, so just leave it at that, and if it's meant to be, he'll come back. Then you can decide if that cunt is what you really want."

Amy was a proper witch. Just as she predicted, he came back, and we went there again for round two (or three or four or whatever number we were on at that point). I was in LA, having a nightcap at the Sunset Marquis, when all of a sudden, someone came up behind me, put his hands over my eyes, and said, "Guess who?" I didn't have to guess because before he even touched me, I smelled him. At first I was extremely cold toward him, but he worked his charming little ways again and what can I say? He and I were like magnets.

He asked me to come up to his room because he wanted to talk to me about something. He showed me his Mickey Mouse underwear, complete with skidmarks, and the family album of photographs he took with him on tour—as intimate as you can get. After what seemed like hours of flirtation on his part, I was about to go home when out came the cherry on the cake: He and his fiancée were expecting a child. My mind went blank and I froze. Any feelings I had ever had for this man went out the window. He was dead to me.

Needless to say, that was our last kiss good-bye.

As much as I've been talked about, you will never hear a story that starts, "Did you hear who fucked Kelly Osbourne?!" I don't go there with many people, and especially not anyone who is going to blab their mouth about it. As experimental as I was when it came to mind-altering substances, I've always been a bit of a prude when it comes to sex (and my vagina is a sacred space, remember?). In London, when groups of girls would get together for a major girl-talk sesh, I was always shocked at how many of them seemed to love doing it in the bum. It was conversation after conversation about bum sex that I could not insert myself into (pun somewhat intended) unless someone wanted to answer my naive questions: "But it's so small! How do you get anything in there? Do you have a big bum hole or something?"

You'd think that in 2017, people would have stopped thinking that if they just married rich, their problems would be over, but there's still a whole culture of women who trade off their looks. Hollywood is ground-zero for women mind-fucking—and actual fucking—men to get what they want. In a Hollywood club, you can sit back and observe and it's like watching the Nature Channel. A girl in a body-con and Blahniks will pick out her prey and go in for the kill. These girls are also more than likely getting paid hundreds per night just to be there. People tend to paint marrying someone for their money as an easy way out, but it sounds hard to me, because it surely involves sucking a lot of dick. To each their own, but that is not the lifestyle for me. As my friend Cher once said, "My mom said to me, 'One day you should settle down and marry a rich man,' and I said, 'Mom, I am a rich man.'"

I have never thought I needed to date anyone rich or famous, but I do want to date someone who has their shit together, who has something going on in their life and wants to make the world a better place. It doesn't matter what he does for a living, as long as it's not illegal and as long as he's interested and passionate about it. Someone who actually wants to work hard. Ambition and willingness to work hard are the biggest fucking turn-ons for me, because I work my ass off to make things better for myself, the people around me, and the world, so I don't want to date someone who just sits around playing with his balls all day. In England, we say someone's "lazy as cunting fuck," which means they're just there to have sex. Needless to say, I'm not interested in those people.

I like my independence. I've worked hard for it, and I intend to keep it, even in a relationship. I want to date someone who feels the same. I can't stand it when a guy is constantly asking me what he can and should do with his life. Do not ask me what socks you should wear. Make up your own mind. One thing I will never understand about men is how they can act so tough, break bones and not go to the doctor, but as soon as they get a simple cold, anyone would think they have the plague. Do not turn me into your mother, because that, to me, is the biggest boner killer.

Just because you're dating someone doesn't mean you have the right to tell that person what to do. You only have the right to say how something makes you feel, and good communication is key. I think we're often fed this fairy tale that relationships just happen, but the truth is quite the opposite. They take lots of hard work, lots of honesty, and lots of talking. People tend to spill intimate details and problems to their friends because they're too scared to bring them up with their partner. How the fuck is that going to help anything? Are you going to have your best friend call your boyfriend to tell him how you feel? It's always good to vent, but if you're not talking about your relationship with the person you're actually in the relationship with, you're not going to get very far.

I don't know if I'll ever get married, and to be honest, I'm not even sure that's what I want. As it is, I've worn enough beautiful dresses and had enough moments that were all about me. I guess I'll just have to keep doing this dating thing, suffer through a few more dick pics, and see where it takes me.

*Love,*
*Kelly O*

# 16 ∗

......................................................................................

# DEAR BULLYING

I wish I could remember our first altercation. However, that would be impossible because I was still in my mother's stomach. Before I even took my first breath. My mother's due date was Halloween. People called me the spawn of Satan and questioned whether I would be born with 666 on the back of my head. I was labeled "Rosemary's Baby" before I was even shat out. Being bullied was just part of my life.

I do, however, remember the first time I was violently bullied. I was maybe five years old, in the park, playing with my brother, on a roundabout. My hair was still golden blond then, and Jack and I were dressed in matching Ghostbusters costumes. As the other kids and I tried to get the roundabout to go as fast as it could, a boy standing on the sidelines said, "Is your dad Ozzy Osbourne?" I said yes, smiling with pride. I swung past him again and he told me, "Well, my dad's Michael Jackson." I was not sure if he was telling the truth or being a little twat, but it was confirmed that he was a twat as my face met his fist and he punched me in my right eye. I had to go to school with a black eye for what seemed like an eternity.

To be called a bully in today's society is a very big deal. The term is often greatly misused to describe anyone doing something that someone else doesn't like. The first time I was ever called a bully, it was in elementary school. It was because I'd told a girl in my class, Jenna, that she had a mustache when she was being mean to Sammy, for no reason other than the fact that Sammy was better at ballet than she was. Of course, she told on me and I got in so much trouble that I got toast. "Toast" was a way worse punishment than detention, because it meant you had to be at school at six A.M. to make toast for all the boarders. It punished the parents as well as the student, but Mum didn't give a fuck and got up and drove me to toast without saying a word, because she knew I wasn't a bully. I knew I wasn't a bully; I just wasn't going to sit there and watch Jenna, who, as it turns out, *was* a bully, destroy my best friend in front of the entire class.

If you are outspoken about your opinions, call people out, or stand up for yourself or someone else, you are not a bully. Bullying is when you choose to hurt someone, and your reasons have nothing to do with them and everything to do with you. Bullying is when someone makes it their mission to take their misery out on you so that they can make themselves feel better about their own shitty life.

The true definition of being victimized by a bully is when a person has done nothing to deserve it and the attackers are just showing off to make themselves feel better about their own inadequacies. It is jealousy and self-loathing in its most hateful form. Having spent so many years hating myself, I'm highly attuned to that quality in others. That's what I see when I look at bullies. I can see in their eyes that they didn't even really want to do what they did, but they had to, because their ego is in control. Ego can be both a beautiful and disgusting thing. You have to have a healthy ego to survive in this world, but the minute you give your ego too much power, you enter into evil, dangerous territory. Ego is a fragile little thing that lives inside you. It loves to be coddled, but if you've got a fragile one that's easily offended, then watch the fuck out, because a hurt ego will try to mend itself by hurting someone else.

I've been bullied at every stage of my life. I'm not trying to make this a Kelly O pity party—I just want to be clear that being famous or being in the public eye doesn't protect you from bullying. In my case, it actually invites it.

I had a grown man throw a bottle at me when I was just a teenager, and I've had girls bump into me, try to pull my hair out, or even jump me in clubs, all in an effort to impress their friends with how unimpressed they were with someone famous. One particular time, when I was about sixteen, I was bullied in a way that could not have been more textbook.

I was at Barfly in Camden, and Fleur and I had gone downstairs to use the toilet. There were two single stalls, and we were both having a wee when a group of girls walked in. They were talking a lot of shit on someone . . . then I realized that someone was me. "Isn't it a shame that Kelly Osbourne is so fat and ugly when her mum's so gorgeous?" one of them said. "If I were Sharon, I would have prayed for Kelly to be stillborn." It was really hard-core.

Fleur and I unlocked our doors and stepped out of the stalls at the same time.

"Isn't it funny, Kelly," Fleur said, looking at me, "that people don't think you have ears?"

"I know, Fleur," I said. "It is funny, isn't it?"

Then we washed our hands—good hygiene even with a looming pack of bitches!—and left. From the looks on the girls' faces, I could tell they were shitting themselves. Since there were only two of them, I didn't really think anything of it, and by then I had learned that this kind of pettiness comes with the territory of being an Osbourne (which I wouldn't trade for the fucking world).

As the night went on, the bitchy bathroom girls had more and more friends join them, and it was a gang forming across the pub. I didn't even notice it until I went to the bar to get a black and cider** and saw one of the girls from the bathroom staring me down. When our eyes met, she mouthed, "I'll get you. What the fuck do you think you're doing?" Still, I hadn't done anything at this point aside from let them know that I wasn't fucking deaf. I got my drink and went back to sit with my friends.

** TRANSLATION

🇬🇧 Black and cider

🇺🇸 Any alcoholic cider mixed with Ribena, a blackcurrant drink

About an hour goes by, and one of my friends went to buy cigarettes from the machine right by the door. This was when you could still smoke in bars, and buying cigarettes was as easy as buying candy. I trailed behind her, not paying attention to anything other than what was right in front of me, because I was absorbed in playing Snake on my mobile phone. I was working on my highest score ever.

The girl in the bathroom was almost a foot taller than I was—she was a proper lass**—so with my face down, I didn't even see her standing there until my shoulder hit hers. I looked up and knew instantly.

*Oh God, here we go.*

The girl reached out and wrapped her hands around my hair. I had these long extensions in at the time and thought, *Go ahead and pull my hair, bitch. It's glued in, it will fall right out.*

My second thought was, *Fuck it*, and I punched her in the face.

The Bathroom Bitch Gang had now grown from two to six, and they all jumped in. I looked over to my right and saw that one of them was going for Sammy, who is the gentlest, kindest person you will ever meet and who had never been in a fight in her life. (For God's sake, she went on to become a nurse and wipes the assholes of senior citizens for a living, because all she wants to do is help people.) Somehow, I managed to jump up and push myself off the wall to get around the girl I'd hit, and karate kick one of the other girls off Sammy.

In the meantime, three of the Bathroom Bitch Gang were on Fleur, who was defending herself to the best of her ability, so I jumped in to make it more of an even fight. That was when Old Bill** drove by, saw a bunch of girls fighting outside the pub, stopped, and put me in handcuffs.

The policeman who had stopped was a member of the K9 unit, who drove BMWs with sunroofs for the dogs. He'd just gotten off duty and was on his way home when he witnessed our scuffle, so fortunately for me, his sunroof was still open on the top of the car he'd just left me in the back of. I'm double-jointed everywhere, so it took minimal effort to slide my arms out from behind my back and under my feet, to allow me to climb out of the top of the car and run back into the club.

Inside, the girl who'd started everything was talking to the policeman and playing the victim.

"This is fucked up!" I told him. "She and her friends jumped me. I had six girls on me at once!"

The bouncers, who had seen everything, came to back me up.

The policeman listened for a few minutes. Clearly, he was wishing he'd never stopped and had just kept on driving. He took off my handcuffs and said, "Okay, I'm going to turn my back," implying that if he didn't see anything, he couldn't do anything, and then turned around and walked out the door. The bouncer looked at me and said, "Go on," then held the girl back and let me knock her one more time.

I could have been a UFC fighter, because when someone comes at me, all of a sudden I go mentally blank and feel no pain. As it turns out, my extensions had not just "slipped right out." When Sammy, Fleur, and I left the Barfly, I realized the girl had ripped three 50p-size[**] chunks of hair out of my head, and that tickly feeling down the back of my neck was actually blood running out of my scalp and trickling down to soak my shirt.

Violence is a disgusting thing, and I do not condone it. I have never started a fight in my life, but I will stand up for myself and the people I love. That's how I was raised. England is a scrappy culture, and you have to prove yourself in certain situations. You have to walk down the street like you're not better than anyone else, but also like you're not one to be fucked with. In certain parts of London, they can smell weakness. All of a sudden, you will start to see them circling. Trust me when I say that you should be scared of British women. Especially the Londoners. They don't give a shit and they will knock you the fuck out.

Not all bullying is the physical kind, though, and at times, bullying with words or by exclusion can be even more hurtful than when someone whacks you upside the head. Especially when you're an adult. Yes, adults get bullied, too, which is unfathomable but true.

Recently, I went through something where there was a growing divide between me and a group of girls I'd always been friends with in London. I'd known that it was happening, but what really drove it home was the realization that my so-called friends were inviting me along only to the events that they couldn't get into on their own. While there, they would also make a point of bragging about all the events they went to together that I wasn't invited to. After turning down a job that would have made me hundreds of thousands of dollars so that I could fly from Los Angeles to London for the wedding of one of my closest friends, I arrived for the ceremony to find out not only that I had not been invited to the hen night**—even though all the other bridesmaids, who I had introduced to the bride, were there and knew I was in town—but also that I was the only one who was staying on my own and not in the prearranged hotel with the rest of "the group."

** TRANSLATION

🇬🇧 Hen night
🇺🇸 Bachelorette party

If someone doesn't like me, I don't care. Just tell me, or don't invite me, rather than putting me in a situation where I'm going to be ignored. What are we, twelve years old? What is the point? The whole time, I was sitting there thinking, *Did I do something? Maybe it was something I said . . .*, when in reality, no, it was neither. It can start to make you desperate, and you'll overcompensate to try to fit in.

In this last situation, everyone was drinking red wine, because it was all there was. Red wine doesn't agree with me and almost always makes me sick, but this night, I thought maybe if I just gave it a try and drank one glass, I'd loosen up and stop feeling so self-conscious. Maybe it's not them, maybe it's me. So I drank a glass, they still ignored me, and I threw up. Bullying by exclusion is a recipe for insanity. It truly makes you doubt yourself and leaves you wondering, *Is it me?* The answer to that question is almost always no, it is not you.

As adults, the workplace becomes our high school. We are forced to spend time with the same people over and over again, regardless of whether we like them. That new girl, the one who was hired for the promotion you didn't get? Well, leaving her sitting at her desk alone eating a sad desk salad while the rest of you go out for lunch is bullying by exclusion. Consistently talking over someone in meetings, stealing their ideas, and trying to make them look bad in front of your colleagues or boss is bullying. So is trying to make sure the people who work for you feel worthless so they'll never feel confident enough to ask for what they deserve or get a job somewhere that doesn't treat them like shit.

The same goes for social media. People like to think that writing mean comments on a celebrity's Instagram isn't bullying, but no—it's still bullying! People don't understand the power of social media and the fires they fuel with their hateful comments. What we say and do online has consequences in real life.

Have you read the news lately? There have been an astonishing number of reports from all over the world about people who commit suicide after being bullied on social media. That does not even take into consideration the situations that go unreported or in which no one was brave enough to step forward and tell the truth.

Bullying always comes back to how the bullies feels about themselves. If you're happy with your life, you won't ever feel the need to go out of your way to try to make someone else feel shitty about theirs.

If you are the victim of bullying, you just have to keep moving forward, and you'll see that the biggest people in your pond are really just plankton in the oceanic scheme of things. It is a cliché, but a true cliché. The nerd who got picked on for four years in high school could easily be the next Mark Zuckerberg of the world. And the pretty cheerleader everyone put on a pedestal could end up alone, without any love or magic in her life, filled with regret as she looks back and realizes she should have been nicer. Once you learn what really matters, nine times out of ten it is too late.

Something that people always told me, which I really only began to understand recently, is that things really do get better. I say better, not easier, because life only gets harder. It's just that you learn to live life to the fullest in spite of this. Bullies will never go away—it's just that we have built the skills and have the power to become more immune to them. If you build your life on positive things, like hard work, love, and trying to be a better person, you can only grow. If you build your life on tearing other people down, you're only going to shrink. I know what I want. Which one do you want?

*Love,*
*Kelly O*

# 17 *

························································································

# DEAR MUM'S CANCER & DAD'S ACCIDENT

Fuck you, and fuck you, too.

You were the two worst experiences of my life.

I had just moved to New York when I found out Mum had cancer—literally just moved. It was the same day. I was going to record my first album, and Mum, Jack, and Aimee had come with me to help me get settled. We were staying at the Trump Hotel, the big gold one that faces Central Park, because they had apartment-style rooms that you could rent for months at a time, and those rooms had computers in them (back then, that was a really big deal!).

That night, I left Jack and Mum at the apartment and went out to dinner with a bunch of friends. Jonathan Cheban and Nicole Richie were there, and we all went downtown to Nobu Next Door. Halfway through dinner, Jack called me.

"Kelly, I need you to come home," he said.

I wasn't having it. "Jack," I said, "if you've just gotten into an argument with Mum and you want me to solve it for you, I can't do that, because I'm at dinner with my friends."

Then he started to cry. "No, Kelly, come home. Mum's got cancer and she's going to die. Dana just called and told us Mum's got terminal cancer." (Dana was our in-house accountant at the time.)

I hit the floor. I was so stunned, I couldn't move.

Nicole Richie—remember how tiny she is—picked me up, carried me out of the restaurant, and got us a cab. I held on to her and sobbed the whole way uptown. Nicole got me back to my mum, and I remember looking at her as she was leaving and seeing that my mascara and the rest of my makeup had smeared all over her Missoni dress. I felt so bad because I knew how much those dresses cost. Nicole never mentioned it.

A few weeks prior, we had made Mum go to the doctor because she wasn't acting like herself. Her skin was gray and she was sleeping all the time. It was weird, but never once did it cross anyone's mind that it might be something as serious as cancer. When the test results came back, the doctor's office couldn't get ahold of Mum because she was traveling. The only person they were able to reach who had authorization to talk to the doctor's office was Dana. She got the news and immediately got in touch with Mum. Her delivery couldn't have been less perfect.

"You've got to come home," she said. "You've got terminal cancer."

Imagine hearing that—from your fucking accountant. When you're all the way across the country.

We were all in so much shock, anxiety-ridden panic, and fear over the possibility of losing Mum that a doctor had to come over and sedate us. The next morning, a family friend helped us get everything together—when we hadn't even been there long enough to properly unpack—and put us on a private plane back to Los Angeles. That entire plane flight, we all held on to my mum so tightly with clenched fists and did not let her go.

Dad was the last to find out, and he will never let us live that down. At the time, I thought, *Well, you weren't exactly in a state to be the one to tell first*, but in retrospect, he should have been. It was his wife, after all. He had a right to know first.

My mum is the center not just of our family but of my entire universe. When I say *family,* I don't just mean Mum, Dad, Jack, Aimee, and me, but also everyone who works with us. Many of them have been with us for decades and have become blood. When Mum went into the hospital, we were all a little lost without her. Shortly after she went, her dog Minnie had to go into the veterinary hospital to be treated for dehydration, because she refused to leave Mum's side to eat or even get a drink of water.

I know that my brother is my mum's favorite, just like I know that I am Dad's favorite. Jack is Mum's everything, and I think that's just how it is with mothers and sons and fathers and daughters. When I look at my friends' families, I see the same kinds of relationships.

Mum's cancer hit Jack hard. He helped out as much as he could, but it tore him up to see her in the hospital and he didn't go visit as much. My sister also tried to help, but we were all scared out of our minds, and Aimee's way of coping was to strictly follow every rule the doctor had given us and tackle everything step by step. If Mum was having a bad day and didn't want to do something, Aimee refused to listen to her. Though all she was trying to do was help take care of Mum, she'd yell, they'd fight, and it wasn't good for either one of them.

Dad went insane. At the thought of losing Mum, he spiraled into heavy, heavy addiction, worse than anything we'd seen in years.

*Okay*, I thought, *I can see how this isn't going to work*, and I knew I had to take care of Mum because no one else could. At the time, I had been given the role of Lindsay Lohan's best friend in *Freaky Friday*, but I backed out. If I had only two years left with Mum, I wasn't going to spend those two years making and promoting a movie. When I picked my mother over what would have admittedly been a great start to my acting career, I got dropped by my agent. At the time, it was the least of my concerns.

We eventually found out that the cancer wasn't terminal, but it was stage three, which meant she had a 40 percent chance of surviving. They weren't the best odds, but we were going to fucking take them, because that meant there was a fighting chance she was going to live. I essentially moved in with Mum, slept on a fold-out bed next to her every night, and even had my own parking space at the hospital.

What I learned most from this whole experience is that love and laughter are the most healing medicines in the world. It was my mission to show my mother unconditional love and make her laugh. She had always called me her little Snow White because of my pale skin and red lips. One day, I dyed my bright pink hair black, put on a bright red ribbon and red lipstick, and waltzed into her room singing, "Someday my prince will come." She laughed so hard she almost wet the hospital bed.

Watching her go through chemo was the hardest part, because she was so sick. She hit her low point and started to give up on herself when she began to lose her hair.

Like mine, Mum's hair is her everything, and her identity. She has always had confidence issues with her appearance, and she changed a lot of those with plastic surgery, but her bright red hair was the one thing she never felt she needed to change. When her hair started to fall out piece by piece, so did her hope. It didn't help that industry people were starting rumors about how Mum was "faking it" as a publicity stunt, which just proved to me how fucked up so many of the people of Hollywood are.

I would do anything for her—and so would most people who know her—so I got the information for Cher's wig maker and had these amazingly perfect wigs made that looked exactly like Mum's natural hair. I took the wigs around and had everyone in the house put them on, so when I gave them to her I also gave her a little photo album of the whole family wearing the wigs and channeling their best inner Sharon.

Mum was losing her fight and had turned her bedroom pitch-black and refused to come out. She curtained off every window and hung a curtain across the room so that when anyone walked in, they couldn't even see her in her bed. She needed another round of chemo, and the last one had been so hard that she didn't think she could do it.

One afternoon, Robin Williams came over to the house, marched right up to her room, and just climbed into bed with her. He stayed in there all afternoon, and throughout the house, you could hear her cackling with laughter. Shortly after he left, she told us that she'd decided she would go back and finish chemo. I tear up when I think about this, because Robin Williams helped save Mum's life and I don't think there are words in the world to describe how much what he did meant to my family. He was a beautiful, generous man.

At this time, Dad was seeing a doctor who had volunteered to put together the team of nurses who would take care of Mum at home while she was going through chemo. While some of them were fantastic and are still family friends to this day, others didn't know what they were doing.

Unfortunately, it was one of the latter who was on duty the night Mum had a seizure. The nurse was running around her in circles, screaming about not knowing what to do. I yelled at her, "Dial 911, you fucking bitch!"

I finally called for an ambulance, and together with the idiot nurse, we got Mum stabilized. I ran downstairs to get Dad from his room, which we called the bunker because you could scream as loud as you wanted in that house and no one would hear you in the bunker.

I threw the door open. "Dad, Mum just had a seizure, the ambulance is on its way." Scared of how he would react, I tried to sound as calm as possible, like everything was under control. "Get dressed, we're going to the hospital!"

I had reason to be scared. Dad was there in his boxers, and I watched him scoop his hand into a bowl of pills, swallow a handful of something, and then wash it down with vodka, like it was water and he was dying of thirst. I didn't know what to do. Maybe he knew what he was doing. Maybe he could handle it.

He couldn't.

Dad and I rode to the hospital in the ambulance. There was a bench seat that ran along the side. I was farthest up, near Mum's head, and then Dad was next, at her waist. Mum was unconscious.

Dad has the biggest hands, like the Thing from the Fantastic Four—I sometimes think that is why he walks the way he does, it's like they are made of stone—and in the ambulance, he leaned over to put his hand out to see if Mum was breathing. Then he passed out with his hand over her mouth, and it looked like he was trying to kill her. The EMTs tried to pull him off, and Dad, not knowing where he was or what he was doing, started to resist out of habit. They pulled the ambulance over and started to call the police.

I can't even accurately tell you what I was feeling in that moment. It looked like I was about to lose everything I loved in one short ambulance ride. I begged the EMTs not to call the police. "Please don't do this," I said. "What do I have left if you do this?" I was sobbing and shaking, scared out of my mind, and the EMTs took pity on me and decided not to call the police, but they said that they were rushing Dad into detox as soon as we got to the hospital. They then handed me two zip-ties and I had to tie those gargantuan hands to a bar along the back of the bench so they could check his vitals and give him oxygen.

Once we were at the hospital, I ran back and forth from the room where my mother was recovering from a seizure to the room where my father was being treated for a drug overdose and alcohol poisoning.

Dad could not handle the thought of losing Mum. He was terrified, and his way of dealing with it was to dive headfirst into his addiction. He was using anything he could get his hands on. Unbeknownst to the rest of the family, Dad was paying an exorbitant amount of money for a "doctor" to come to the house and shoot him up whenever he wanted, while the man's son sat in our dining room and played video games on a handheld Nintendo. I know that Dad asked for everything he got, but any doctor who was worth the paper their prescription pad is printed on should have recognized this kind of behavior and had the integrity to say no rather than accepting the check.

By now, it had been two years of this routine and Mum had only three chemo sessions left. We were waiting to hear if she was in remission. My album *Changes* had just come out, and for the first time in longer than I could remember, I felt optimistic. Maybe life wasn't going to be such shit anymore.

I was wrong.

For the album, Dad and I had recorded a version of one of his Black Sabbath songs, "Changes," together, and we'd gone to England to promote it. Dad didn't want to do the press day. The way I see it is that my dad is the head of the family. He's given us all so much that if he doesn't want to do something, one of us will pick up the slack. I said that was fine, that I could do it by myself.

I was appearing on *Richard and Judy* in England when everyone off-camera started frantically trying to get my attention and motioning for me to get up and walk off live TV. What was going on? As soon as I stepped out of the shot, someone handed me a phone. It was Mum in Los Angeles.

"Are you sitting down?" she asked. You can guarantee it's not good news when someone asks if you're sitting down. Especially when you've been pulled off live TV and you are a member of my family. It was then that I noticed there was a policeman in the room. "Mum," I asked, "why are the police here? Have I done something wrong?"

"Kelly, listen to me," she said, and I could hear the seriousness in her voice. "That policeman is going to be taking you to your father. He's had a bike accident and they don't know if he's going to make it. I need you to go there, and I need you to sign the paper. I know that you're scared, but I need you to get to that hospital."

I ran out of *Richard and Judy* without even getting my purse. I took a police car to a train, then another police car to another police car that took me to the hospital, all in the hopes that we could keep what had just happened out of the press long enough for the family to figure out what the fuck was going on.

As soon as I got to the hospital, they threw me in a room, washed my hands, and put me in scrubs with a mask over my mouth. Then they walked me into intensive care, where Dad was lying in a hospital bed. I could hear him talking. Screaming, actually: "Push the morphine button! Push the morphine button!"

*He's going to be okay*, I thought. *He's going to be okay.*

I asked him what happened and if he was okay. "Kel, I love you," he said. "No matter what happens, I love you . . ."

Then I heard this noise that sounded like gargling, and brown bubbles started coming out of his mouth. My father had broken all his ribs, and the ribs had punctured his lungs. At this point, his lungs were filling with blood and it was coming out of his mouth. Every machine in the room gave off a high-pitched *beeeeeeeeep*. The doctors rushed in and performed a procedure that required a "flushing" of blood. From my hips down, I felt warm . . . I didn't realize it right away, but the warmth I was feeling was actually my father's blood. I started to scream as the nurses shoved me out of the way.

He flatlined in front of me.

In these kinds of moments, it's strange how your brain reacts and what you remember. All the nurses who were there happened to be male, and I remember thinking how they looked like staff at a mental institution.

*Oh*, I thought, *they're going to take me away and put me in a strait-jacket.*

Instead of locking me up, two of the nurses took me by my shoulders and led me out into the hall. My heels dragged on the floor and I was fighting to go back in to be with my dad.

Dad had been riding an ATV at our house in Buckinghamshire when it rolled and landed on top of him. It broke his collarbone, a vertebra in his neck, and all his ribs.

I sat in the waiting room in intensive care with Mum on the phone and people from the hospital standing in front of me with a bunch of papers. They were release forms saying I authorized them to do whatever they needed to do to save my dad's life but that I wouldn't hold them responsible if they killed him in the process. I was the only person there who could sign them. I was nineteen.

I didn't want to. "I can't sign this! It's not okay if he dies!" I cried, while Mum was yelling at me through the phone from Los Angeles, "Kelly, you have to do this! Sign the fucking papers right now."

I signed, and within seconds, they wheeled Dad past me into surgery. They had resuscitated him, and he was yelling, "Don't fuck up my tattoos! I'll fucking kill you if you fuck up my tattoos!"

That gave me a little bit of hope.

I stayed in the hospital, in my bloody clothes, for more than twenty-four hours, but I had no real concept of time. With everyone being so busy, and figuring out the time difference between LA and London, everyone had understandably forgotten about me. Finally, Mum asked where I was, and someone—I was honestly in such a state that I can't even remember who—came, picked me up, took me home, and put me in the bath.

As soon as I could, I went straight back to the hospital. After the surgery, Dad was in a medically induced coma with machines breathing for him. The doctor said to me, "The surgery went well, but your daddy is not out of the woods."

"He's not fucking Goldilocks!" I snapped back. I was so angry at everyone who wasn't Dad. I sat there every day and just talked to him over the in-and-out *whoosh* of the breathing machine. My half brother, Louis, came to the hospital, to my rescue, to be with me, but neither one of us could keep it together. Seeing Dad like that . . . he'd always been so invincible. He was our hero, and now we might lose him because he wasn't out of the goddamn woods yet.

Mum and I swapped. She came to London to stay with Dad, and I went back to Los Angeles to fill in for her at work, because she was doing *The Sharon Osbourne Show* at the time. Marilyn Manson was the guest that day, which made it tolerable, since I was at least working with someone I knew well. As soon as I was done, I flew straight back to London, and two days after I returned, after fourteen days in a coma, Dad woke up.

He still couldn't breathe without the machine, and he couldn't talk, but he was conscious of everything around him. Our song had gone number one all over the world, everywhere except America, and it was his and my first number one hit together. He just kept holding his finger up, the number one, and crying.

Once Dad was able to breathe on his own again, they took him off the machines. It took him a couple of weeks to remember everyone else, but he knew who I was right away. Ha-ha, fuckers!

I took him cheese and onion sandwiches and trifle, his favorite dessert, every day, and I knew he was going to be okay the afternoon I showed up to see a bedpan go flying out the door of his room and hear him scream, "I can wipe my own fucking ass, thank you very much! Fuck off!"

When he left the hospital, he didn't want a nurse, so I helped as much as I could, just as I'd done when Mum was sick. I helped him brush his teeth, and I'd put on a swimsuit to help him shower twice a day.

Dad recovered, and eventually, I did, too. I've no doubt that it took me longer. I wouldn't go through those years and those events again for anything, but that was really when I learned how strong my family is. There is no denying that we are fighters through and through.

We haven't always gotten along, and each one of us is crazy in our own way, but despite the circus that we may appear to be from the outside, you will never find a more loyal family than the Osbournes. No matter what they might do that I disagree with, or what happens to us as a whole, my family is my world. I would do anything for them, and I know they would do anything for me. As my sister has spoken about publicly, we are not close. Still, if anyone ever said anything negative about her, I would rip their fucking head off. Loyalty takes work. It means showing up for people even when it's not convenient or easy for you, but it is the most important thing. Loyalty is how you build a foundation for your life. Without that foundation, anything you build will come crashing down the first time something comes along and shakes it. But when it is strong, you'll be amazed at just how unshakable you are.

 *Love,*
*Kelly O*

# 18 *

## DEAR LYME DISEASE

I think it is time people finally know about our relationship and the real reason behind my seizure. You ruined my life for more than ten years and almost killed me. Thank fucking God you're gone, because if you were still here, I probably wouldn't be.

When I was diagnosed with you, I didn't even really know what Lyme disease was. I thought I got it because there was too much limestone in our water in England. As soon as it was explained to me how people really do catch it, I instantly knew where I'd gotten it: from a tick in a fucking reindeer sanctuary, the kind that we just so happened to have in the back garden of our family house in England.

There were reindeer all around our house in England, and Mum has these photographs of us as little kids, running in a field surrounded by reindeer, and we looked like little angels, which we were because we still had not been exposed to the cruelties of the world. At one point, she even convinced the family that Dad would want a reindeer sanctuary on our property, so to "surprise" my dad for his birthday, we had this giant reindeer pen built. Mum kept saying, "Your father is going to love this!" On the big day, we were all excited. We blindfolded Dad and walked him out to what honestly turned out looking rather grim and foreboding—but he was going to love it!

As soon as we removed the blindfold, Dad took one look at this "gift" and said, "What the fuck is this? It looks like a concentration camp."

It was at such a sanctuary that I was bitten by a tick. I saw this fat, gross bug buried halfway into my skin, screamed, and ran to Dad, who burned it off with a match. Everyone knows now not do that, but back then we didn't. I forgot about the tick almost as soon as it was gone, but it left me with a painful reminder: Lyme disease.

Unfortunately, I wouldn't know this for almost another decade, and during that time, my body and brain disintegrated. I knew that something was wrong with me, but I didn't know what, and no one in my family believed me.

I had what my doctors called "traveling pain." One day my throat would hurt, the next day my stomach, the day after that my joints. I was tired, and not the kind of tired that comes from staying out too late the night before—this was pure exhaustion. I'd wake up in the morning and feel as though I were encased in cement. The irony of this was that a lot of the time, I was in too much pain to even sleep. I felt as though I'd been hit by a bus and had whiplash: It hurt to walk, to turn my head, or to raise my arm to get something off a shelf.

I'd wake up some mornings and not understand what had happened in my sleep. My mouth would be all bloody, and the sides of my cheeks were lined with ulcers. *What the fuck is wrong with me?*

I'd have crazy mood swings, totally fine one minute and sobbing the next, but everyone kept writing them off: "Oh, Kelly's having another wobbler, is she?" I went to doctor after doctor trying to figure it out, but they all kept insisting there was nothing wrong with me. I don't blame them—I had been self-medicating for so many years that no one trusted me. Mum didn't know what to believe: Was I really in pain, or was I just trying to get someone to write me another prescription?

Then came one of the scariest moments of my life. I had a three-and-a-half-minute grand mal seizure.

If anyone still thought I was fine, they didn't after that.

I was on the set of *Fashion Police*, and the cameras were rolling. I started to sweat. In a matter of seconds, my clothes were soaked through and my makeup was dripping off my face. I looked at Joan and said, "Joan, something's not right . . ."

Then all of a sudden, my arms shot up like a T. rex and my head twisted to the side. Melissa Rivers was there that day, and the last thing I remember is her saying, "Oh my God, she's having a seizure!" She knew what to do and grabbed me and got me down on the ground in the fetal position.

One of the last things I remember was someone trying to shove a fat Louis Vuitton wallet in my mouth, and Melissa started yelling, "Don't put anything in her mouth! Just keep her on her side and her chin up." When someone is having a seizure and they're on their side, if they start foaming at the mouth, it will keep them from choking. If they're on their back, with something in their mouth, they can choke to death.

Thank God Missy was there that day, because she probably saved my life. I was foaming, and I'd bitten down so hard that I'd torn up the inside of my mouth, a flashback to those mornings of waking up and not knowing what had happened. When I finished seizing, I stood up and said, "Let's finish the show, guys!"

It was like I was drunk—my vision swirly and my brain loopy— and I looked like a vampire with blood running down the sides of my mouth. Someone asked, "Do you know where you are?"

I was offended. "Of course I know where I am," I said. "I'm in the country riding horses with my mum! Let's get back to work!"

In the almost six years I'd worked with Joan, she had never missed a day, so even in my sickest state I didn't want to let her down. But there was no finishing the show that day, and an ambulance rushed me to the hospital where I again became unconscious.

The seizure had scared Mum to death. I was unconscious and Mum had my power of attorney, so she signed papers allowing any kind of treatment the doctors thought necessary.

A brain scan showed scarring on my brain, which suggested I had been having seizures for an unknown amount of time. They diagnosed me with epilepsy and put me on a brain tranquilizer called Keppra to prevent any more seizures. You lose your driver's license when you have a seizure, and you have to be seizure-free for a year before you get it back, but even if I'd had my license, I couldn't have driven anywhere on Keppra.

The doctors kept changing my prescription, trying to get the dosage right, and it turned me into a zombie. You know in movies where a mental patient sits in a rocking chair in a cardigan and nightgown and stares at a wall all day? That was me. I lost me in every way you could imagine. I had about two hours a day where I was functioning, and that was it.

I couldn't work out, couldn't go out with friends, could barely even hold a conversation. The only work I could do was *Fashion Police*. I'd time my two hours of life to coincide with that, and for the rest of the day, I was pretty much a goner.

My prescriptions kept piling up. Every pill I took had some kind of a side effect, and then I was given another pill to take care of that side effect. I couldn't sleep, so they gave me Ambien. When Ambien made me nauseated, they switched me to Trazodone, but that gave me acid reflux, so then I had to take an antacid every day. One of the medications made me break out in a rash, so then there was an ointment for that. I took cranberry extract and antibiotics because one medication made me prone to getting urinary tract infections. Painkillers—for an ex–painkiller addict—to help with the head- and body aches. I was having panic attacks because I was so scared of having another seizure. Not kidding—I had pills to deal with the anxiety that I was having from taking so many pills. I had so many pill bottles that I had to get a separate bag for them. It was even bigger than my makeup bag, and the bottles rattled so much when I walked that it sounded as though I had maracas in my purse.

At this time, I was engaged and living with my fiancé, and my disease wasn't easy on either of us. I'd always been very independent in my relationships, and it was important to me to maintain my own life, but now that was impossible. He didn't want to let me out of his sight for fear that I'd have another seizure when I was alone. He drove me to doctors' appointments and helped me remember what pills to take. We were in our twenties but living the life of a couple in their eighties.

When I got yet another prescription that left me barely able to speak, I was reduced to a lump on the couch, and that was my break-ing point. I took my bag of pills, and my fiancé drove me to my mum's house. Since we didn't live together, she hadn't seen the full amount of everything that I'd been prescribed, and she didn't realize that I was taking dozens of different pills every single day. I sat them all out in front of her, one by one, until they lined up the length of the counter. "I can't live like this anymore," I said. "When have you ever known me to not want to take a pill? I'm a vegetable. I have no life."

"Oh my God, Kel," she said. I started to cry, and she did, too. As a last resort, she called Philip Battiade at Infusio.

Philip is an alternative medicine practitioner, and I'd first met him when he treated my brother for MS. Later, Philip told me he'd been confused by my behavior at our first meeting and that he and his partner kept looking at each other like, "What's wrong with this woman?" I'd been extremely chatty—which is pretty normal for me—but I'd repeated myself over and over again and kept asking questions that made it seem as though I hadn't been following any-thing anyone else said.

My odd behavior had led my family to believe that I was using again, but when I met with Philip, I assured him that I hadn't used unprescribed drugs in years and that I thought I had Lyme disease. I had started entering my symptoms into online quizzes, and the results kept coming back Lyme disease, Lyme disease, Lyme disease.

For the first time in all my conversations with doctors, someone listened to me, and I got tested. The results were positive: I had stage three neurological Lyme disease. I was relieved to finally know what was going on, but I was also scared shitless. The disease had progressed so far that I was about six months away from having a heart attack or ending up in a wheelchair. To get my disease into remission, I needed treatment immediately.

The rigorous shooting schedule of *Fashion Police* meant that it was almost impossible to get time off, but the producers agreed to give it to me under one condition: that I pull some strings and get the show an interview with Miley Cyrus. Fortunately, Miley agreed. We did the interview, and the next day I got on a plane and flew to Philip's treatment center in Germany.

My fiancé went with me, and I remember writing in my journal and ordering drink after drink as he slept beside me on the plane. On one hand—maybe this was crazy. On the other—I was falling apart and had never felt so crazy. I didn't have a choice.

My one alternative was intravenous antibiotics, which is the type of Lyme disease treatment that is approved in the United States. With this kind of treatment, you are basically embalmed for twelve months. Between the drugs I'd taken as an addict and the drugs I'd taken after my seizure, I already felt as though I'd lost years of my life. I wasn't ready to give up another year to pills, needles, doctor's offices, and hospitals.

Within twenty-four hours of arriving at the clinic in Frankfurt, I started stem cell therapy.

Rather than trying to kill off the disease with antibiotics, this treatment worked to strengthen my immune system so my body could fight off and get rid of the disease on its own, which is a much more complete and lasting cure.

I stayed for two weeks of treatment. When I left, I was already feeling better. Within a three months, I started to feel like myself again. The fog had lifted. After six months, I felt healthier than I could ever remember. I still wasn't the fittest athletically, but the muscle aches, joint pain, headaches, nausea, and mood swings were all gone. I was experiencing emotions and feelings again. I'd been in a diseased and doctor-approved drug-induced haze for so long that I didn't know what it was like to be happy or sad or in pain. I didn't even think I had feelings; everything just kind of hummed along at the same level of daze.

I've kept quiet about my Lyme disease not only for fear of pharmaceutical companies coming after me because of the cure I found in Germany but also because it seems like the trendy disease to have right now, and I'm tired of seeing sad celebrities play the victim on the cover of weekly mags. Since I know firsthand how awfully debilitating it is, I know who really has it and who is just trying to prolong their fifteen minutes. I don't understand how anyone could think that the life you have to live with Lyme disease is glamorous.

The harsh truth is that I was able to cure my disease because I had the money to do so. I had the resources to find the right doctors, fly to Germany, take time off work, and invest in alternative therapies. I had loving people in my life who supported me through all this, even when it was fucking miserable to be around me. Most people do not have this, and the way the health care system in the United States works now, they are going to suffer for it.

I strongly believe that the real reason so many alternative therapies that are available elsewhere in the world aren't available in America isn't that they're not safe but that the pharmaceutical companies don't want anything cutting into their profits.

The United States is a country dependent on drugs. Now we have an antidepressant that you take with an antidepressant to make your antidepressant stronger. We also have a new sleeping pill that you can take with your sleeping pills to make your sleeping pills stronger. There are fucking drug ads on TV that all end with the line "May cause death," but doctors keep writing prescriptions and people just keep taking them, no questions asked.

Due to the things I have been through in my life, and certain conditions I struggle with—such as PTSD, ADHD, and anxiety—I will probably always be a person who is on medication. I don't love this fact about myself, but as with many things in my life, it is what it is. I want to be a happy, healthy, functioning person, and for me, this is what it takes. I learned the hard way to do my own research about everything now, and it takes a lot to even get me to pop an ibuprofen.

I've learned to advocate for myself when it comes to my health, and I trust my intuition. If I think something is wrong, I refuse to let anyone dismiss it.

And sadly, I stay the fuck away from reindeer.

*Love,*
*Kelly O*

# 19 ∗

## DEAR DRUGS & ADDICTION

When will people finally understand that you are not cool, nor do you discriminate by race, gender, ethnicity, or birthright? There is nothing glamorous about doing drugs or being an addict. You destroy people, break up families, and take lives. You are the lowest of the low.

This is a hard letter for me to write, because I don't ever want to play into the misconceptions. I am not proud of my past, and I always worry that even talking about you furthers the misconstrued ideas and romantic delusions that a lot of people have about drugs. Whether it's movies like *Scarface* that make drugs seem like a party (at least at first), war stories from rock stars (like my dad), or people coming back with fun fables from their nights out, there's a lot in our culture that teaches us that drugs are fun and that using them is a way to be cool and fit in. Even among addicts—people who should know better—there's often a pissing contest about who popped more pills, who snorted more lines, who got the most fucked up and survived. It drives me crazy, and I don't ever want to be a part of it again. Drugs are all fun and games until somebody dies. It's as simple as that.

I don't know how I survived my years as an addict/self-medicator, emotionally or physically, and when I finally checked into rehab, the doctors didn't know, either. When Dad healed from his accident, we did genealogy testing on our whole family. The results showed that Jack, Dad, and I all have a gene that makes it so we metabolize narcotics and alcohol faster than most people. This, it turned out, was why I could be barely five feet tall in heels and still hold the record for taking the most shots in one night at Bungalow 8: It was literally in my genes. My limits were high, but I still pushed them, and the only reason I'm still here is pure, stupid luck, if you can even call it that.

I've lost a lot of friends to drugs—some who inevitably overdosed after a long history of abuse, others who were just trying something for the first time. More than a decade ago, a good friend of mine died from taking half an Ecstasy pill. When he started to throw up, his friends were too scared to take him to the hospital, and to this day, my heart breaks when I think about it.

While I am not in AA or another program, I take all mind-altering substances very, very seriously. Alcohol is a drug. Weed is a drug. The pills the doctor gives you are drugs. You think you're better than a crackhead because the drugs you use come with a prescription? That's a laugh. An addict is an addict is an addict, and a drug is a drug is a drug. And if you think your status makes you immune, think again: While people discriminate, drugs and drug dealers do not. It doesn't matter if you're rich, a celebrity, or a gutter punk, a drug dealer just sees you as a nose or a vein or a mouth. I can't stand this new cult of go-greeners who are like, "I only drink organic juice! I'm, like, so offended, I can't believe you don't compost!" Then snort-snort-snort. I'm sorry? How many people had to die from drug warfare just so you could sniff your line? You just go green with your bad self and take a shit on your compost pile for me.

I had always said I was never going to do drugs—"Never ever, not me, blah blah blah." I had learned to identify the different stages and signs of addiction by the time I was seven years old. When we lived in the Palisades, I remember Dad once putting on a suit, complete with a red silk shirt, and ordering a white limo because he wanted to take the family out to dinner at Lawry's Steakhouse in Beverly Hills. Sounds nice, right? Except no one had planned to go out that night. It was already close to Jack's and my bedtime, Mum wasn't ready at all, and Dad was screaming at us to get in the car. I knew immediately that this meant he was drinking again. For fuck's sake, my father, the Prince of Darkness, was in a white suit serving up some real *Saturday Night Fever* on a Tuesday. By the time I was a teenager, I could look at his handwriting and tell what drugs he was on—I wanted it to be sloppy, because that meant it was booze. If his letters were neat and tight, that meant something far, far worse.

However, I don't blame Dad for the fact that I ended up a drug user, nor do I blame growing up in the public eye. For me, drugs were a coping mechanism that also fueled my self-destruction. I put most, if not all, of the blame on myself, combined with a little bit on some of the things that I was going through at the height of my use.

As a user, I was what is called a trash can, someone who'd do any- and everything. I can honestly say that the only drug I have never done is crack, but like I said before, big fucking whoop. It's a small distinction.

The first time I ever used anything that altered how I felt was when I was twelve and we were on a family vacation in Hawaii. There was one beach where all the kids would hang out, and someone there gave me a shot of vodka. It gave me the spinnies and made me feel ill. Jack was there, and he'd apparently been drunk before, which made him an old pro. Jack took care of me and walked me back to the hotel. I didn't love alcohol from that first sip, but I didn't hate it, either. To this day, I still feel that way.

In Los Angeles, we lived at the Sunset Marquis for a while, and to this day, that hotel is my Cheers, the place where everybody knows my name and every naughty thing I've done. The staff called me the Eloise of the Sunset Marquis, and though I never ordered a single raisin from room service, I knew everyone from the general manager to the groundskeeper, who no longer has me nagging him to let me help feed the bunny rabbits that were all over the property. Now he has Pearl nagging him for fish food to feed the koi.

I found other ways to work, though. There was a tree conveniently positioned right outside the window of my room, and at night when I was supposed to be in bed, I'd sneak out, climb down it, and—a preteen in my cloud pajamas—head straight to the bar (where there's now a large black-and-white photo of my father hanging, but it wasn't there in the nineties). I'd take up my usual perch behind the bar, tucked in among the ice trays, and clean and polish the glasses in exchange for a Malibu Pineapple. In retrospect, what the fuck were the bartenders thinking?! In that moment, it was really fun and I got to know everyone who came through the bar.

When I was thirteen, I had my tonsils taken out and the doctors gave me a prescription for liquid Vicodin to help with the excruciating pain as I recovered. That started my first true love affair. After that, I would have had my tonsils out once a week if it would have gotten me more Vicodin. When I took it, it was like all my problems faded into the background, which in turn made me forget about the physical pain I was in. Even though other people probably saw me as slower and less fun to be around when I was on it, it made me feel confident. The relentless screams of my normal insecure chattering were silenced. Instead of feeling different and out of place, like I normally did, I felt like part of the crowd, like everyone liked me. I became the life of the party, in my own head, of course.

I wasn't going to let these feelings go just because my prescription had run out, so I got more. It was way easier than it should have been. I was an anxious kid, so doctors were always writing me scripts. I would say that they handed them out as freely as candy, but they probably would have been stricter with Fruit Gums and Maltesers** than they were with Klonopin, Vicodin, or Valium.

** TRANSLATION

🇬🇧 Fruit Gums and Maltesers

🇺🇸 British candy

I thought those pills were magic. They shut off my feelings and welcomed me into a state of what I believed to be peace. This felt good when I was a teenager full of feelings, and I figured that if taking one felt good, taking ten would feel amazing. I was too naive to really understand what I was doing. I think I can tell you now that it was far from peaceful. Everything I was taking was basically synthetic heroin, I just thought it was okay because, well, doctor's orders. On the rare occasion when the doctors wouldn't come through, there was always the world's easiest pharmacy, also known as your parents' medicine cabinet.

Everything got worse as I got older. *The Osbournes* had thrust Jack and me into the spotlight, and I don't think either one of us was really prepared for it. We were suddenly treated like celebrities everywhere we went, even though we could not figure out what we had done to deserve the attention.

We were children, but being famous meant that people treated us like adults. We lived close enough that we could walk to the Sunset Strip, so we could tell Mum we were going for ice cream and then pop into the Whisky or the Rainbow Room. Soon we were regular club kids. With that came party drugs, which were a whole new world for me. I remember once being at On the Rox, the bar above the Roxy, and watching a very famous, and supposedly very clean-cut, all-American pop star walk in, dump a bunch of coke on the bar, cut up some lines, snort them, and then turn around and walk right back out. My mind was blown. *She does that?!* I thought.

Jack and I were a team and adversaries at the same time. I had a hard time being the protective big sister, as I found it disturbingly disgusting to watch grown women throw themselves at a sixteen-year-old boy because he was on TV. It never failed to piss me off. Since I was his big sister, I tried to be protective of him, which never failed to piss *him* off. Then at other times, as my brother, he'd try to be protective of me, and you can guess how well I took that. Soon, we were fighting all the time and having epic showdowns that often made it onto episodes of the show.

We were both strangely quiet about drugs, though. I knew that he was starting to use them, and he knew that I was starting, too. Even though we got them from the same person, I can't recall us ever using together. We never even talked about it, and the understanding was unspoken: The most important thing to both of us was that no one tell Mum and Dad.

I already had a fucking five-star education on how to use drugs and how to hide them, because I'd seen it my whole life from being on tour and the world I'd grown up in. I cannot stress enough that it was not my parents' fault—we were protected to the best of their ability, considering the world we lived in. We always had an adult with us wherever we went, and they talked to us about drugs. But what else were they going to do? Lock us in a room, like every day we were in a new prison in a different state or country? Or leave us home, so that we saw Mum and Dad just a few weeks out of the year? Absolutely not.

One time, before I had ever even touched a drug, Mum went so far as to make us take a "drug test" when we were at a tour stop in Florida. It was a pregnancy test. We knew because we could see, from where we were sitting, that the box was still in the bin.** I took one look at it and thought, *Yeah, I'll piss on that. I'm a virgin. I'm not fucking pregnant.* Also, I hadn't done drugs yet, so I kept wondering, *Is it Aimee or Jack? Aimee or Jack?* I never did find out, but one thing we did find out was that we were definitely not pregnant. Thanks, Mum. I hope that was a weight off your shoulders.

** TRANSLATION

🇬🇧 Bin

🇺🇸 Trash can

Jack was never as good as hiding it as I was, though, and I was starting to worry in a real way, as hypocritical as it sounds, because I was more than likely worse.

It was time for me to tell Mum that I was worried about Jack. However, I must be honest: As concerned as I was for my brother's health and safety, I'd be lying if I didn't tell you that I shone the spotlight on him so I could keep up with my dirty work in the shadows. As a result of this, I will always feel likely I betrayed both of us by not shining a light on myself as well. It was one of the hardest decisions of my entire life, but I made the right decision. For Jack, treatment worked. He was still underage at the time, which meant that he had no choice but to stick it out with the program and attend every meeting, counseling session, and activity that was suggested. It saved his life, because he's been sober ever since. He's an incredible father, and he's a testament to how a program can work if you're willing to work with it. He was one and done with rehab, whereas it took me a lot longer to figure it out. Like four rehabs, six detoxes, and one mental institution longer.

Drugs are escapism. They allow you to not feel your true feelings and instead feel the ones you think are more fun. Or they erase all feelings, good and bad, so you're just left with nothing. That's what I was going for—total emotional emptiness, any way I could get it.

I never really liked party drugs. There's a ritualistic romantic notion about cocaine, which to me is just boring, sick, and passé. Coke isn't glamorous—it's gross. Though I have done it, I will never understand the desire to go out and do cocaine, because the first thing it is going to do is make you take a shit in a public place. Or you're going to do coke with your boyfriend? So sexy! By the way, coke dick is limper than whiskey dick. He's never going to be able to get it up.

I can't stand Ecstasy. I don't want to touch people, and I don't want to have people touching me. I'm a very loving person, and I tell the people I love that I love them all the time. I don't need to be on something like that that makes you want to stretch out of your skin to do it.

I tried meth once because someone told me it was coke. It was the most disgusting feeling. I ended up cleaning my entire apartment with a toothbrush because I'd sneezed and thought maybe a tiny speck could have fallen out of my nose, and if my dog found it, she would lick it up and then die. After staying up all night scrubbing, I had to get up the next morning and work fifteen hours. I felt like shit.

Even though I preferred to do drugs by myself, I still shared with others. Since I was famous, I couldn't go to a dealer myself, but someone was always willing to do it for me in the hopes they would get some for free in return, even though it was never discussed. After I paid for everything a couple of times, people just expected that was how it worked, and soon I had no shortage of "friends" who were always around. At least until the drugs ran out and we couldn't get more. Even at sixteen, I knew these kinds of people weren't my real friends and that they really didn't give a fuck about me, but I didn't give a fuck about them, either. There was an unspoken mutual arrangement here—they helped me get the drugs and I helped pay for them. Whatever this was, it was certainly not friendship.

The ones who could afford their own drugs but just hung around me because I was famous were sometimes even shittier. I remember once being in the car with a certain celebutwat (who shall also remain nameless) when she called AJ McLean of the Backstreet Boys. He'd been in and out of rehab but had been sober for a while at the time, and she put him on speakerphone. "So, AJ," she said in a fake-sweet voice. She told him who she was and then went on to tell him, "I think you need to relapse, because you haven't been in the press in a while and people are going to forget about you." He stammered a few words, not sure if she was joking or not, and I remember sliding lower and lower in the backseat, feeling what an unthinkably horrible thing that was to say to an addict.

When Mum got sick, and especially after Dad had his accident, pills became my way of coping. I had one parent battling cancer and the other in a coma. I'd wake up every day in a new kind of hell, one that wouldn't let me crawl back under the covers and hide. I had to make phone calls, sign papers, talk to doctors, console family members, and, at nineteen, make adult decisions that would have been hard for someone three times my age. The only way I could even face my life was by opening that pill bottle, shaking out a few pills—or a handful—into my palm, and throwing them down my throat. When the numbness started to kick in, then I could get out of bed. When you take an Oxy or Vicodin, it's not like your pain suddenly goes away; you just forget about it for a bit. It makes the hell you are living in go from searing hot to lukewarm. Although it is a different temperature, it is still hell, just a hell of a different kind.

Finally, I was so fucked up that I couldn't hide it anymore, and my parents decided I was going to rehab.

This was the beginning of a process that would ultimately take five painful years. It was a violent cycle. I'd get to a point where I'd see sobriety on the horizon, then something would happen and I'd go right back to drowning my despair with pills. It wasn't pretty. In the beginning, I didn't want to stop using. Then I did but still wasn't strong enough to quit. I was such a selfish fuck-up, I thought, that maybe I didn't have a right to be happy.

I thought no one else was like me in my addiction, and that no one could possibly understand what I was going through. I was wrong, and when I look back, I can see that I was just being selfish. That selfishness was born out of shame, and it is something that all addicts have in common. I felt a level of shame that, unless you have been there yourself, you could never comprehend, and that's what made me, and what makes every other addict, so self-serving. I felt very sorry for myself, so in little ways, here and there, I justified everything I did, because I'd do anything—abuse, lie, manipulate—to try to get rid of this fucking awful, shameful feeling.

I think I only truly started to heal when I began to see the difference between shame and embarrassment. Embarrassment is a raindrop or a lonely tear, whereas shame is the whole fucking ocean. Embarrassment was what I felt when Mum deliberately knocked someone's toupee off at a Royal Family dinner in England and then ran off, leaving me there to pat it back on, saying, "Sorry, sir! Sors . . ."

Shame was the inner voice telling me that I was fat, stupid, worthless, and didn't deserve to be alive. Thankfully, through years of therapy, rehab, detox, and a lot of hard work, I finally got that voice to shut the fuck up.

 *Love,*
*Kelly O*

# DEAR REHAB

You and I first became acquainted when I was one day old and Dad checked into the Betty Ford Center, where I would go visit you, a mere babe in Mum's arms, for the first three months of my life. You became a more important part of my past when I was nineteen. That is when we got hot and heavy for about five years, but now I am very proud to say I don't know you anymore.

My first trip to rehab at nineteen was a literal trip, after I was so fucked up that I fell down in the living room floor and all my drugs came spilling out of my bag.

With pills rolling everywhere, my parents realized I was a mess. They decided I was going to rehab, something we knew all about, since, as I mentioned, Dad had checked into the Betty Ford Center the day after I was born. Still, I didn't know what to expect for myself. As soon as it dawned on me that this was really happening, I grabbed handfuls of pills, whatever I could find, and swallowed them.

I figured it was my last chance. I might as well go out with a bang.

My parents then threw me into the back of an MTV production van, where the crew covered me with a blanket so they could sneak me past the crowd of paparazzi outside our house and take me to Promises Treatment Center in Malibu. I completely blacked out and didn't come to until after I'd pissed myself in a chair in the waiting room at check-in.

As I woke up and looked around, I thought I was tripping because I could hear my parents' voices. Little did I know they were coming from the TV, because they were on *Larry King Live* at that very moment. They'd gone on the show to promote the third season of *The Osbournes*, but instead they were talking about how I'd gone to rehab when I hadn't even made it past the front desk.

I was covered in piss and angrier than sin.

It took me a long time to get over that. When I saw Mum and Dad talking about me on *Larry King Live*, I thought they were trying to show the world that it wasn't their fault. I was already hurt because it seemed as though it had taken forever for them to step in and say, "Hey, we love you and don't want you to die. You have to stop this."

I'd always thought I was a bad liar, so I was angry that no one had seen what was happening and that it had taken this long to get to this point. *Fuck you, Mum and Dad!* I thought. *I'm here in a living hell, and you're on TV trying to prove you're not bad parents?*

Now that I've grown up, I see what they did for what it really was: their way of owning their responsibility and trying to protect me and the family when I was in such a fragile state. What else were they supposed to do?

Mum had practically invented the art of feeding stories to the press, and she also knew this was something we could hide for only so long. If she and Dad broke the news, it was our story, and not one for the tabloids to break. By being open about my self-medicating, they were telling the world that they were standing by me. They weren't ashamed of me, and I shouldn't be ashamed of myself, either.

I didn't really pick up on that message at the time. "This is all your fucking fault!" was practically my mantra. It wasn't their fault, though. They didn't put the drugs in my mouth, they didn't give them to me, and now they were dealing with it in the best way they knew how. I was scared and angry—not just at my parents but at myself, the media, everyone I knew, basically the entire world. I was throwing a fit because I didn't want to live life on life's terms—I wanted to live them on mine.

What were my terms? Well, for starters, I wanted to be a totally different person and never have to deal with anything that hurt or was difficult. Tough shit—we all know that was never going to happen.

Promises had a reputation, but it wasn't a very good one. It has since overhauled itself a lot and become a respected facility, but back in 2004, the joke was, "Promise promises we won't stay sober." It was a hotel without a bar and people checked in and out of there like it was the fucking Four Seasons. It had a red tile roof, fireplaces, and two different pools. If you felt like it, you could hit golf balls off into the ocean, get acupuncture or a massage, or work out with a personal trainer.

I'd been taking so many pills that I started to go into withdrawal almost immediately after I arrived. For the first three hours, I just sat there violently shaking, like I was in the middle of an earthquake that no one else could feel.

Even then I knew I wasn't going to stay sober. I couldn't wait to get out and do drugs again. I was simply playing the game and biding my time.

I honed my lying skills on the therapists and nurses, even getting one doctor to write me a prescription for Klonopin because I convinced him it would help me kick my synthetic heroin addiction. Let me put it this way: Klonopin makes Xanax look like Benadryl.

I didn't know how serious my drug use was and I didn't understand what I was doing to myself. Drugs were my safety blanket, and I didn't want that taken away. I was in mental pain because of what my family and I were going through, and I was also in physical pain because, though I didn't know it at the time, I was suffering from undiagnosed Lyme disease. The symptoms varied from day to day, but the constant was that I felt like shit daily. I'd forget words or names that I used every day. When that stuff happened, I'd feel stupid, like maybe I really was as insignificant as people thought.

I had no idea what was going on, and with Mum in the hospital with cancer, I didn't feel as though I had anyone I could talk to about it. I just knew that drugs helped me get through the day, and so I was not giving them up. Now I can honestly say that I don't know if my drug use would have gotten as bad as it did if I wasn't trying to run from the effects of Lyme disease, but like I've said, the past is the past, and I'm not trying to tempt fate or blame anyone, or anything, for what I did.

Addicts and treatment centers often say once you've been to rehab, whether you were ready to go or not, it changes you. It's true. Even if, like I did, you don't try to quit and you only half pay attention, you learn that there is a way out—if you want it. You never drink or use the same way again. You will always see your conscience at the bottom of every glass, pill bottle, or baggie. You start to think that maybe this isn't the only way.

Rehabilitation can fall under so many umbrellas, but it's basically breaking yourself down and then building yourself back up. You can see why that's so hard. First off, you have to be honest with yourself and everyone in your life, and the last thing an addict wants is honesty, since the foundation of who you are is based on lies.

Addicts are so used to lying, manipulating, and believing what we want to believe that we've often forgotten what it's like to be straightforward with anybody. We'll lie even when we don't have to, because we're just so used to doing it.

When I was in treatment, the people who got through to me the most were the group counselors, not the doctors or therapists. The group counselors were almost always former users who were now sober. With addicts, it takes one to know one. Whereas you might be able to tell a few sob stories and drum up some sympathy from a doctor, a former addict is not buying your bullshit. They know all the signs, and believe me, you come up with some shit when you are getting sober.

There was no placating me, no "yes ma'am"ing me, just the truth, told kindly and persistently over and over again. "Kelly, you are killing yourself. Is this what you want? What do you think your life will be like if you keep using? Do you want to keep using? Is this the kind of life you want for yourself? The only places left for you are prisons, institutions, and death."

This approach, over time, began to break the drug shell I had built around myself, the one that convinced me I was so unique that no one else could ever possibly understand what I was going through.

The first phase of rehab is the physical detox, where your body is in shock because it's become chemically dependent on the drugs that have suddenly been taken away. I puked, I sweat, I shook. I had no control over my body. My arms shot out and my legs kicked in a spasm of twitches. I finally discovered what "kicking the habit" really meant.

I swore that if something would just take away the pain that I was in at that moment, I would never touch drugs again and would devote my life to doing something good. That was one second, and then the next, all I wanted was my drugs.

I honestly can't count the number of times I detoxed, because in addition to my trips to rehab, I also did several home detoxes so the media wouldn't find out I'd relapsed again. Detox is not something I got better at with practice. Each time, it hurt just as much physically and even more emotionally, because I knew that the last time I had done this, I swore it was the last time. *Get through this,* I would have told myself the last time, *and you'll never have to detox again.* Yet there I was, detoxing. Again.

People typically spend thirty days in rehab, but I think it should be at least twice that. Most people don't really even start to come alive until the second or third week. A physical detox can take anywhere from one to four weeks (or longer), and I didn't even begin to know who I was or where to start until the chemicals had left my system. Once I did start to figure out who I was, I didn't like that person. In fact, I despised her.

Almost everyone goes through the same stages in rehab. First, I was pissed off. I'd think, *I don't want to be here* or *I'm not meant to be here. I'm not like these fucking people.* Good rehab facilities make everyone share a room with another patient, and they strip everyone of all their comforts. Everyone has a roommate to remind them that we are equal in our addictions, and it was a constant flow of people coming and going.

Eventually, the anger wore off. I submitted to where I was, and then my true sadness took over. I did not want to be a part of anything, but I would still go and sit through the therapies, because I did not have a choice.

I had been in a cloud of fucking chemicals for so long that I did not remember what it was like to feel. Then all of a sudden, I would feel everything. I was fresh, raw, and incredibly vulnerable. I had to learn how to be a person again. I realized that I was there, so I might as well start talking. I had plenty to talk about, too. I had been in limbo for so long that my life had filled with unattended problems that got worse and worse every time I decided to get high instead of dealing with them.

One of the hardest things about rehab is that I was suddenly in an environment where everyone was telling me what to do. No matter who I was outside of rehab, in it, I felt like I was treated like a child. Everything is scheduled, from the alarm that goes off in the morning to a mandatory lights-out at night. Most facilities are set up so that men and women are treated completely separately. At my last rehab, if I so much as looked at a guy, I would get written up and be cleaning the toilets before I knew it.

That is because they were trying to protect me from myself. When my body was coming off drugs, my hormones went crazy trying to regulate themselves again. Most addicts, myself included, are as emotional as teenagers in this stage, and then throw in the fact that a lot of addicts just switch addictions. They can come off drugs and move on to sex without skipping a beat. I am so grateful that I didn't get that, because I've seen how much it hurts everyone involved.

I met a lot of amazing people in rehab, who listened to me and cared about me in ways that no one in my regular life did, but I'm not going to write about them here. Though I am not in the program anymore, I stay true to and uphold the principles that gave me life again. Narcotics Anonymous, Alcoholics Anonymous, and Al-Anon are all *anonymous*. Attending meetings and listening to other people tell their stories helped me realize I was not alone in my problems, but I typically do not share in the meetings. I did once, after a lot of urging from my sponsor at the time, and talked about things that were happening with my family. A few days later, that story ended up in the tabloids.

I don't know who in the group leaked it or what—if anything—they got from doing it, but I think that's about the lowest of the low. Needless to say, I have not shared since, but it also reaffirmed my belief that I would never gossip or share someone else's story outside a safe space, in any way. For me, what happens in meetings stays in meetings.

I cycled in and out of rehab from the time I was about nineteen until I was twenty-four, and tried other things as well. Mum once locked me in a mental institution for three days, and it scared the hell out of me. People were endlessly playing checkers (I don't know why this is a thing in mental institutions, but it is) or in straitjackets, rocking back and forth and screaming. I had to wear paper shoes, since I could potentially kill myself with a shoelace, and wasn't allowed to have anything metal, not even a spoon. I wasn't suicidal by medical standards, but I heard Mum's message loud and clear: Stop using drugs before I was gone for good.

At one point, I moved to London, because at the time, my drug of choice was unavailable there. I pretty much kicked the habit on my own and was happier than I'd ever been before, because I finally felt like I was my own person. Then I moved back to LA so that we could start filming *Osbournes Reloaded*. As soon as I was in the land of yoga pants and palm trees, I fell right back into my old habits. I was trying to kill myself, though I wouldn't have admitted it if anyone had asked me. Every day, I was taking more and more pills, hoping that I wouldn't wake up. I joked that the only friend I had was Jesus, my Domino's Pizza delivery guy, except that it wasn't really a joke. Most days, he was the only person I saw because I barely left the house and just stayed inside doing drugs all day. Using drugs had never been so depressing, because now I knew who I was when I was off them. I wanted to quit. I really did. I just wasn't strong enough yet.

I'm no stranger to an intervention. My family has gone through about ten of them with my dad, and I've also been through them with friends. So when a guy showed up at my house and said he was there for my intervention, I knew what was in store, and I hated him immediately.

Now, at this point, I was ready to quit. I really was, but I was also so, so angry. I knew I had a problem, and again, I found myself in a selfish train of thought, wondering why it had taken everyone around me so long to help.

When I kick off, you cannot stop me. I went ballistic and made the intervention guy stand outside while I screamed and yelled inside. Mum called the cops, and when they showed up, they felt sorry for me. Instead of arresting me, they gave me their business card and said to call if I ever needed anything. After that, I made everyone leave the house, then fell to the floor and sobbed. I do not know why or how, but in this I managed to have one second of clarity that spiraled into shame. Why was I blaming everyone else for what I was doing to myself? Finally, I packed my suitcase and let the guy with the clipboard take me to rehab. I was ready to go.

Eventually I stopped hating Clipboard (I won't say his name, because I want to respect his privacy. As you can imagine, what he does is very sensitive and confidential, and I would never want to violate that) and he became a close friend and a pillar of support. Years later, when I broke my foot and a doctor wrote me a prescription for painkillers, I turned it into a piece of art and gave it to Clipboard, a little memento of gratitude to him from his most difficult client (a title that I still hold today).

On this trip, I went to Hazelden Betty Ford's Springbrook center, outside of Portland, Oregon. It saved and changed my life. It was finally where I learned how to differentiate myself from my family. There, I learned that structure, schedule, and rules really do work for me, and when I left, for the first time ever, I felt equipped to live life on life's terms, even though I was terrified.

What finally made my last trip to rehab successful was that I learned that you cannot just treat your addiction and leave your other problems out to fester and rot. It's a constant healing process. I'd been to therapy on and off since I was a kid, but at twenty-four, it started to make a difference. I read a book, recommended to me by my therapist, called *Facing Codependence* by Pia Mellody, and something clicked. I finally understood my life and my feelings, and that realization was so freeing. Now that I knew what I was dealing with, I could work toward solutions.

In a dysfunctional family that is dealing with trauma or an active addict, everyone has a role to play. That role is often different from the person they really are. In my family, I was the fuck-up daughter. That was how everyone saw me. They got uncomfortable when I asked them to see me as anything else. Eventually, I stopped asking. Even though Fuck-up Daughter wasn't the part I would have chosen for myself, it was the part I played. When I finally learned, through lots of therapy and reflection, that this was just a character and not who I really was, it was like I'd finally been handed the answer to a question I hadn't even known I was asking. The term *codependent* clicked and made sense in a way that *addict* never had.

I've never been 100 percent comfortable with the wholesale label *drug addict*. My issues have always been complex, not totally black-and-white—I've had periods of heavy drinking and drug use, but when I was in a good place emotionally, I could have a glass of champagne or two, and then head home to go to bed early. True addicts have lost the power to choose whether they use. It's a compulsion, like OCD. They feel as though they have to do it or they will die. That was never me, but I still didn't understand why I kept ending up back where I'd started.

On my last trip to rehab, I finally learned that I couldn't heal my addiction without healing my dysfunctional relationships. Growing up with an addict as a father, I'd become used to one-sided relationships and putting my own needs last, both of which are classic codependency traits. That's why, when I was happy and getting over my addiction on my own in London, I gave it all up and moved back to Los Angeles as soon as I was asked, even though I knew it would be bad for me.

Through therapy, I started to learn how to set boundaries and to ask for what I needed without feeling guilty. I had to say, "I love you, Mum, I love you, Dad, but I have to start living my life for me now. It doesn't mean I respect you any less, because I respect you more than anyone else in the entire world, but I can't do this anymore."

I also encouraged them to set boundaries with me. One outcome of this was that we made a rule with one another about being late. We would wait no more than twenty minutes, because we were all so busy that sometimes we wouldn't realize we'd double-booked, and leave the other person waiting for hours. That meant that even if you show up when I'm leaving, I'm still leaving and you can't be mad.

Drugs are no longer my coping mechanism. Now I manage pain through creativity, friendship, and self-care. The crazier my life gets, the more focused I become on the things that make me feel good. I'll write or make mood boards for my next clothing collection. I make sure to talk about what's going on and how I feel about it, rather than keeping it all to myself. I go to the gym or do yoga. After so many years of feeling sorry for myself and being selfish, I now get satisfaction from doing things for other people. Whether that's helping to spread the word about a cause that is important to me or babysitting Pearl so Lisa can have the afternoon off, it makes me feel good and reminds me that I have more love in my life than I do problems.

Rehabilitation is a never-ending process, and I'm still working on myself. I know what works for me and what keeps me in a sane place where I can be happy and productive. For the first time ever, my life is manageable. I see a therapist, and I will continue to do so because I truly believe that only crazy people do not go to therapy.

I still struggle to accept who I am and the life that I was born into, but I'm learning to be more patient with myself and with other people. I'm different, and yeah, I shouldn't have seen a lot of the things that I saw, but you know what? That's life.

We move on.

Everything that happens shapes you into who you are.

I'm proud of where I am and what I went through to get here.

 *Love,*
*Kelly O*

# 21 *

·····················································

# DEAR BODY

I love you and I promise to take care of you. I bet there were quite a few years when you never thought you'd hear me say that, let alone actually do it.

Going back to the beginning of this love/hate relationship: The joke in our house was always that Dad hid his drugs in the oven because that was the last place anyone in the family would look. Except it wasn't a joke because it was true—there wasn't a whole lot of cooking going on in our house.

When we were on tour, we mostly ate catered food. In some cities, the catering would be amazing, but in most it was whatever could be prepared easily to feed a thousand people. The bus kitchen was just a microwave, so as you can imagine, fresh salads and homemade meals were not in abundance.

When I was growing up, there weren't a ton of working mothers, and if there were, they certainly didn't work as hard as ours, so I think Mum felt a lot of pressure. Whenever she thought there was something she couldn't teach us, whether that was because of her schedule or because it was something she didn't know much about, she didn't expect us to just figure it out. Instead, she'd leave it to the professionals and send us somewhere where we could get the information.

This was how my brother, sister, and I found ourselves sitting in a nutritionist's office. I was ten and hated that woman immediately. The first thing she did was ask to see my nails, to check if I had a calcium deficiency. I didn't even know what calcium was. Then she asked me if, when I took a shit, was it a floater, a drifter, or a sinker? I didn't know! I was doing most of my dumping in truck stops—I wasn't stopping to study it! I was mostly worried about whether I'd found a bathroom with a locking door.

That woman wanted to talk about shit, and she was full of it. Everything she taught us was about counting calories, the same kind of super-restrictive stuff you read on pro-ana websites, like, "If you're eating a salad, always get the dressing on the side. Make sure it's fat-free, and then dip your fork in the dressing before you pick up the lettuce." Can you imagine telling a kid that? You'd send them straight to counseling. Even at ten, I called BS on the whole thing and didn't follow her rules.

For most of my life, nutrition wasn't something I thought about. I didn't understand fruits or vegetables, and the concept of a healthy lifestyle was completely foreign to me. I didn't know how many calories I was supposed to eat in a day. Instead, I just ate when I was hungry and didn't eat when I wasn't.

I wasn't a fat kid—until we moved to America. There's just a lot of shit in American food that isn't good for you. For example, in England, I can drink as much milk as I want. In the US, I'm lactose intolerant. It wasn't like my body started changing in weird and unexplained ways. It was simple: I just got fatter.

I started to get teased at school, and kids would call me "Smelly Kelly with the big fat belly," but that was nothing compared to what people in the media said. Imagine waking up, getting the newspaper that's been shoved through your letterbox, and opening it to a picture of you with a headline that reads "Ozzy Osbourne's Beached Whale of a Daughter!" When you're sixteen fucking years old! When it came to the media, I was bullied way more for being fat than I ever was for being a drug addict and going to rehab. After all—beautiful people go to rehab all the time, so it was almost culturally acceptable. Being fat was not.

My weight struggles continued into my early twenties, and my parents tried to help me, or at least make me feel better about myself. Mum would always give me some sort of encouragement about how I was different and beautiful in my own way. Dad was no less caring, though not exactly tactful like Mum.

One of my all-time favorite Dad-isms happened once when I was in my early twenties and in the middle of doing a medical detox at home. I was coming off a really heavy opiate habit, and coming off hard. Dad came in and sat on the edge of my bed. He'd been through his own share of detoxes, so he knew the hell I was going through. Bless his heart, he tried to make me feel better.

"Kel," he said, "is this because you're fat? If it is because you're fat, I'll pay for you to get a personal trainer if you want. I really love you, and I don't want to see you like this."

I was sweating and had the kicks, and my whole body was in pain. I just looked at him, and then rolled over and faced the wall. Part of me wanted to laugh, but the other part thought, *I'm fucking dying here and you're asking me if it's because I'm fat?!?* I do love you, Dad!

I hated working out, and when I couldn't comfort myself with drugs, I turned to the next best thing: food. It was a potent combination, and I soon hit my heaviest point. It wasn't that I didn't want to lose weight; it was more that it just seemed overwhelming. I didn't like the way I looked but didn't know how to fix it. *I need to lose fifty pounds—where the fuck do I start?!* What was more, I didn't even like myself enough to try.

All that changed when I went on *Dancing with the Stars*.

In London, I had auditioned for a role in *Chicago*. I'd poured my all into the audition, even going to a ballet store beforehand and buying a leotard and cutoff sweatshirt. I was still all chubby and even more butch than I am now, up there in a *Flashdance* rehearsal outfit. No one who I was auditioning for had ever heard me sing live before. I sang "Funny Honey," and when I finished, the room was dead silent. *Well, shit*, I thought, *I guess I've really fucked this one up.*

Then, after a beat, everyone jumped up and started cheering. "You've got it!" one of the producers said. "You're our new Roxie!" I nearly shat my leotard—I couldn't believe they were giving me the lead!

They rushed me straight into rehearsals, and after an hour, the choreographer—who I dearly love to this day—addressed the elephant in the room. "Uh-uh, honey," he said. "I can't teach this one to dance." Bob Fosse is all hips and jazz hands, and I just thrashed around like I was being electrocuted. I couldn't even do a box step, and in Broadway productions, a box step is as basic as walking.

I ended up with the role of Mama Morton, and at twenty-two, I was the youngest person to ever play the role in the West End. Doing live theater ended up being one of the most thrilling and challenging experiences of my life.

I still knew I needed to learn how to fucking dance, though, so when the opportunity came up to do *Dancing with the Stars*, my chubby ass pulled the leotard out of the closet and went for it. It was the best thing I've ever done for my health.

I can honestly say that Louis van Amstel changed my life. He was one of the first people in my entire life, outside of my family, who was 100 percent there for me, and it wasn't just about the show. He truly believed in me. That's a feeling too few people in this world ever get to feel. It was fucking amazing. I have to give credit where credit is due, because without him, I wouldn't be where I am today, and I didn't make it easy on him.

I showed up to my first day of rehearsal on an empty stomach. I hadn't eaten anything beforehand because I wasn't hungry, and so halfway through, I puked. Louis took one look at me bent over a trash can and sighed. "This is going to be a tougher job than I thought," he said. "I see we have to start from the beginning and get the basics down before we even teach you how to dance."

**✳✳ TRANSLATION**

🇬🇧 Petrol
🇺🇸 Gasoline

The first thing he did was teach me to think of eating as putting petrol** in your car: Your car won't run without fuel, and it also won't run if you put the wrong kind of fuel in it. He taught me how to eat mostly lean protein and vegetables— as opposed to fat and carbs, which were what I usually ate—and to adjust how many calories I ate according to how much I practiced.

I had always hated working out, mainly because I hated sweating.

I've worked out with my mum and her trainer before, and it's so hard-core. I'll look over and Mum's barely broken a sweat, like she's walked under a mister at most. Meanwhile, I'm dying and look like I've just been dunked in a pool. When Dad works out, he's the same, so I know where my sweat gene comes from.

The sheer physical exercise of *Dancing with the Stars* wasn't the hardest part of it, though. The hardest part was being forced to look at myself in the mirror all day long. Finally, a friend had enough of me. "I'm sick and tired of hearing you talk about yourself this way," she said. She made me promise that I would stop; then she made me stand in front of the mirror and say "I am beautiful" ten times in a row while looking. I couldn't do it to save my life.

"I'm . . . ugh . . . er . . . booo . . ." Finally, I stammered it out, and the more I said it, the easier it got. I even started to believe it. Kind of.

My friends know that if I make a promise, I will keep it, and so that's what I did. Every morning, before I went to rehearsal, I would stand in front of the mirror and tell myself I was fucking beautiful. Sure, it felt silly, but it also worked. Instead of looking at my reflection as I normally did, just looking for things to hate and that I thought were ugly, I started to find things that I actually liked.

For instance, I noticed that I've got really, really long bottom eye-lashes. *Well, that's kind of cool*, I'd think. *Not many people have that.* I'd always really liked the color of my eyes, and I'm one of the few girls I know who's never had a nose job. My jawline might make me look like Winston Churchill and his dog, but it's all part of what makes me *me*.

None of these realizations were easy. As women, we're told so often we should hate ourselves that finding something we like almost makes us feel guilty, but eventually, I got through it. For the first time in my life, instead of just wishing that everything was different, I started to work with what I had.

When I was on *Dancing with the Stars*, losing weight wasn't my goal. Winning wasn't my goal. My main goal was just to get better each week.

Ballroom dancing was different from anything I'd ever done before. I'm a power chick, which is frowned upon in my industry (it's frowned upon in most industries), and ballroom dancing was all about letting the male be in charge. I'd never let anyone lead me before, in anything, but if I didn't do it in this case, I'd be on my ass. At first, it was really, really hard to not be in control, but as my trust in Louis grew, the thing I feared actually became freeing. We were truly a team, and it was a huge weight off my shoulders to know that it wasn't all on me, that I could let someone else take over without everything falling apart.

Being on the show taught me dedication, and it showed me that I could do anything I wanted if I put my mind to it. I never thought I'd do ballroom dancing! Much less be good at it! But I was, and when Louis and I came in third that season, I was so fucking proud. The audience had watched me through the entire show. They'd seen how I'd improved and how hard I'd worked—this was not a victory that people could write off by attributing it to the fact that I was Sharon and Ozzy Osbourne's daughter.

Over the course of the show, and our days of up to fourteen hours of rehearsal, I lost almost fifty pounds, which is a lot for someone my size. I started to notice it first in my chest. I could see my collarbones, then some of my ribs. When I first saw the beginnings of a six-pack, I threw my Spanx in the garbage. *Good riddance*, I thought. Whenever I gain weight, it goes to my boobs first, so much so that people have claimed over and over that I've had a boob job, but this time, I lost almost three cup sizes. No one commented specifically on my shrinking cleavage, but I learned that everyone is absolutely obsessed with weight loss.

The reactions that I got after I was on *Dancing with the Stars* were some of my main prompts for wanting to write this book. Everyone kept asking, "What's your secret?!" as if I fucking had one!

*You watched my transformation on TV!* I thought. *You told me you voted for me! It took months of nonstop dancing, and you're acting like it happened overnight?!* It blew my mind, but I was ignorant to how it looked to people from the outside. It was my life, so I watched every ounce sweat away, but other people were just picking up bits and pieces here and there—that I used to be fat, and now I was skinny. They didn't realize how long it had taken me, but there is no fucking secret. I just worked my ass off, and had the stress fractures in my feet to prove it.

When it comes to weight loss, there is no quick fix. It's not about dieting; it's about diet. You have to overhaul your entire lifestyle. I believe that you should never deny yourself anything, because that's how you end up eating a whole cake while you're trying to limit yourself to forkfuls of lettuce dipped in fat-free dressing.

I used to do whatever I could to avoid working out, and now I get excited about feeling the burn. I love cardio and will mix in yoga and Pilates to keep myself from getting bored. Throughout my process of learning how to eat right and exercise, I was confronted time and time again with how many of the ideas I had about my body were just flat-out wrong. I'd always thought of myself as naturally chubby and someone who just couldn't lose weight—it turned out I'm actually the opposite. My weight still fluctuates—mainly because my schedule is always changing, and sometimes I can't take care of myself as well as I should—but when I am working out consistently, with or without a trainer, I drop weight really fast. I've had to learn to be careful, because now I like working out so much that I can do it too often, and before I know it, I'm too skinny.

I never thought *that* would be my problem, but when I look at pictures of myself at my brother's wedding, I think, *Eat something!* I looked like Skeletor. My body doesn't look good really skinny. It just doesn't, and that's another lesson I had to learn: It's not about weight, or size, but being healthy. My proudest body moment was being on the cover of *Cosmopolitan UK*'s body issue, and they didn't airbrush a thing except for the spots from where I'd gotten waxed the day before and it pulled my spray tan off. (In the UK, there is a law against air-brushing in certain situations, particularly having to do with beauty and aesthetics.) I didn't look like Gisele, but I looked pretty fucking good, and what was more, I looked like me.

Everybody on this planet was put here for a reason, and everybody is uniquely different. Not everybody looks the same. I don't understand this culture we are living in where everyone has the same eyebrows, the same ombré hair, the same bag, the same shoes . . . everybody wants to look the same. Why do you want to be a clone? Why not just be yourself and look like you?

I do think this is changing, but it's mainstream culture leading the charge, and Hollywood is struggling to catch up. If you look at advertisements right now—like the Big Lots commercials or the Progressive ads that star Flo—you'll see women who are beautiful in a real-woman-you-might-actually-know kind of way. They're not stick-thin anorexics, they're not perfect, and they're not trying to be. People want people they can relate to, and they want to look at someone they can easily aspire to, not images that will always be unrealistic and out of reach.

The way most celebrities look is unattainable for most people. Even if someone is famous because they make albums or movies, when they're not doing that, they have to spend all day in the gym with a personal trainer. They get up at four thirty every morning and never get to pick what they eat. Do you think they want to do that? No, they have to. It's part of their job, and it's expensive!

I refuse to fall into this trap that society has set for us. I won't follow these rules and I won't apologize for it, either. Everyone knows what I look like, and everyone has an idea about who they think I am. I'm not going to spend twelve hours a day in the gym trying to get people not to talk shit about me, because I've learned that they're going to talk shit about me no matter what.

My career has never depended on whether I was fat or thin, or whether I'm attractive. I've never made money from my body or from being known as the pretty girl. I've made money because of my opinions, my personality, and hard work, and the longer I'm in this business, the more I realize how rare that is.

At the time of this writing, I am thirty-two, and I'm watching a lot of my friends in the industry go through this awful time with their careers (and sometimes their personal lives). When youth and beauty have been the cornerstones of your life, there's always someone behind you who's younger and prettier. It's enough to cause a nervous breakdown, and I've witnessed dozens of them. I honestly feel for my friends, because it must be awful, but since I don't understand it, I don't know how to help them.

I think the world is cruel to women, no matter how attractive you are. For most of my life in the public eye, I never felt any pressure to be or act sexy, but all that changed when I lost weight. The first time I did a photo shoot in a minidress, rather than loving how I looked, I didn't feel like me and I was super-uncomfortable. Each new look was shorter and shorter, and the photographer kept trying to coach me into "sexy" positions, like with my mouth open and thrusting out my cleavage. Eventually, I cried, doing my drag-queen cry where I bend over so that the tears fall directly onto the floor and don't muss up my makeup—but still, not exactly the lusty vibe they were going for.

That was my biggest failing on *Dancing with the Stars*. Whenever a dance required me to act sexy and like I just couldn't wait to tear that costume off Louis, I'd just freeze up and couldn't do it. Being sexy in front of a crowd is not my thing. I've never aspired to be a sex object, and I used to be a real nerd about it, but now I just do not give a shit anymore. I don't know how I got to the point where I am comfortable embodying my inner sexy for photo shoots or a role, but I am. Aside from that, I do not think I would ever have the confidence of Mae West, if you know what I am saying.

I was blond for a bit as an adult, and one of the main reasons I ditched the golden tresses was that I hated the way people automatically sexualized a skinny blond woman. It was like I'd gone from being a Cabbage Patch Kid to a Barbie. I'll never forget running into a friend at the PETA awards, shortly after I'd gotten skinny. This was a man who'd known my father for years and had watched me grow up. I had on a dress with cutouts, and he was standing next to me and put his arm through one of the cutouts, so he was just standing there holding my naked waist. I made excuses and backed away as quickly as I could, feeling gross and thinking, *Well, he just revealed himself as a pervert.*

That was the first time this happened, but unfortunately it was not the last. At the time I was too surprised to know immediately what to do, but now I call people out on it, and say something: "Excuse me! I just watched you realize I'm not a kid anymore and sexualize me immediately! Do not do that!"

I've spent a lot of my life wishing I looked different, but now I realize that every woman, no matter how beautiful she is, still has to put up with a whole bunch of shit. One of the reasons I stopped covering the red carpet was because I could no longer stomach it, standing there with a smile on my face while watching successful actresses get grilled with the most asinine questions.

No one—*no one*—asks a man what he's wearing to the Oscars, because it's probably the same tux he wore to the last awards show. Instead, it's serious questions about his films or other very important projects he's working on. Meanwhile, every single woman gets asked about her dress and who made it—nothing about her achievements, what she's working on, or any nominations that brought her to the show that night. I was constantly shocked by how stupid the questions were—I've seen people ask an actress what she did to get in shape for the big night, which is code for asking her how she lost weight—and from three feet away, I could see these women's faces fall, how it was obvious that they weren't happy but had to answer anyway to avoid seeming like a bitch.

How you look is important to your self-esteem—I wouldn't have a career in fashion if I didn't think that—but I think we as a society have to stop telling women that how you look is the most important thing. It's toxic, and we're raising a generation of girls who are incredibly harsh on themselves. When I was a teenager, I was definitely bullied some for being overweight, but for the most part, none of my classmates gave a fuck about how I looked.

I think that's different today. While I was working on this letter, I was staying with my dear friend Kelly Cutrone in New York and had the chance to spend tons of time hanging out with her daughter, Ava, and some of Ava's friends. They are total badass bitches, but they enlightened me to their world, and it ain't pretty. They told me that because of social media, it's all about looks. You can't just look okay; you have to look perfect. They go to SoulCycle every day, they worry about wrinkles, they know girls who get boob jobs and nose jobs—and they're fourteen fucking years old!

I am all for plastic surgery—as Joan said, "My nipples will never be introduced to my belly button"—but I think it should be illegal for children under age eighteen to get it unless it's absolutely necessary. Plastic surgery can change people's lives. I've seen friends turn into new people after a confidence boost from a nose job, or women cry because they were able to go for a jog for the first time in their adult lives after having a breast reduction. But these were adults. Everyone goes through an awkward phase, and your face and body change as you get older, but the way we live now, no one can stand to be imperfect even for a minute. All these young girls feel so much pressure to look a certain way that it's created a toxic cycle of hate and criticism that you direct at yourself and other women.

I get Botox twice a year, and I started in my twenties. Producers, cameramen, and stylists were always asking why I looked so pissed off, even though I'd swear up and down that I wasn't. Then it hit me: I had frown lines crosshatching my forehead from squinting into the bright lights to read the monitors, and it gave me raging resting bitch face.

That's where Botox has helped me, but I always get sad when I see women who look like ventriloquist's dummies because their chin is the only part of their face that moves. I completely believe that people can get addicted to plastic surgery, because suddenly feeling pretty is a thrill. But like anything that gives you a rush, it doesn't last, and soon you need a lot to feel anything at all.

It's a losing game, because if someone loves you for how you look, that's not real love and it will fade no matter what you do. What's inside you—your mind and soul, your sense of humor, and your intellect—is more important than what is on the outside. Superficial beauty fades, and no matter how much Botox or how many butt implants you get, no one is going to find the fountain of youth. Eventually we're all going to look like California raisins with gray hair.

I finally became comfortable with how I look through therapy and just growing up. Once I wasn't a teenager in my me-me-me phase anymore, I was able to really look at other people and see that our true beauty lies in our differences. I also saw that no one is immune to insecurities and occasionally feeling bad about themselves. Even supermodels—and I know quite a few personally—have good days and bad days. Sometimes those bad days can really take over. I still refer to myself as an FFP (Former Fat Person) because I still have that little devil on my shoulder calling me chubby, who wants me to see myself not as I am but as I was.

I don't want to be the most gorgeous woman in the world (sounds boring), but I do want to be content with myself. Feeling good about yourself is also an ongoing process. You're never going to be fixed, and you have to keep working on yourself. It's like when you go on a diet, lose a whole bunch of weight, and then think you can eat whatever you want because you're skinny now. Next thing you know—diet again! You have to make a full life change to eat right, exercise, and be kind to yourself, and you have to commit and stick to it.

It's a lot harder to look in the mirror and say, "I'm beautiful," than it is to pick out all your flaws, but hating yourself will get you nowhere. You have to learn to be confident and not listen to what other people say, because they're just directing their own hate at you, and most of what they say is stupid anyway. If you want to change your life, change it, but remember that the only thing you really have to be is you.

*Love,*
*Kelly O*

# 22 ✳

.......................................................................................

# DEAR MOUTH

On occasion, you've gotten me into real trouble. Sometimes you've spit out utterly the wrong words. But I am not racist. Never have been, or will be.

The first time I ever heard the N-word was my first day of school in America. I was in second grade. As per usual, I didn't fit in with anyone, and as I bumbled through my day, overwhelmed by being a new kid in a new school in an entirely new country, someone called me the N-word.

Though I could tell it was supposed to be an insult, I didn't actually know what it meant. Not only had I never heard the word before, I had never even been exposed to the concept. I decided to ask Mum about it as soon as I got home. I remember it so clearly. We were moving into our house in the Pacific Palisades, and Mum was decorating the house, so everything was MacKenzie-Childs. There were checkerboard teacups and decorative fish adorning the headrests of our dining room chairs. She and I were standing on the steps outside, when I said, "Mum, I have a question. What does n— mean?" The word wasn't even out of my mouth before her hand whipped up and slapped me on the arm.

"Don't you ever say that word again," she said. My cheeks turned as red as her hair. The look on her face at that moment was one of total shock, and she was looking at me like she didn't even know me. I burst into tears and immediately ran upstairs to my room. I had no idea what I'd done, but I knew I'd rarely ever seen Mum that mad before.

Shortly thereafter, I think she realized that I must not have known what I was saying, because she drew me a bath and knocked on the door of my room to apologize. "Where did you learn that word?" she asked. I told her that was what someone at school had called me.

The more she explained what it meant, the more confused I got. Why had they called me that, and furthermore, why would they call anyone that? It didn't make sense to me that someone could dislike someone else for something that they were born as and couldn't change about themselves. Not liking someone because they acted like a total cunt—*that* I understood. Not liking someone for the color of their skin was ridiculous to me. I'd never heard of it before. The whole idea made me sad and filled me with questions and confusion.

Mum must have realized that, because she spent the rest of the day talking about it with me and trying to explain to the best of her abilities. We finally got to the point where Mum couldn't answer my questions anymore, and later that week, she had me watch *Roots*. If that miniseries was supposed to clarify anything, it didn't. "Why did

Kunta Kinte get put on a ship and taken away from his home and his family to go be with people who didn't like him?" was what I wanted to know. This very quickly became an obsession for me. Shortly thereafter, I discovered Martin Luther King Jr. and did my first report at this same new school on him. This was the only way I knew how to tell the other kids in my class that I thought what they were saying was wrong, without fighting.

America is an advanced country in so many ways, but I think it still has a long way to go when it comes to treating people equally and recognizing racial differences and equality. When I see so many white people who don't check their privilege and open their eyes to the fact that the world is rapidly shifting to one that no longer revolves around them, it actually makes me feel embarrassed to be white.

No one has any control over where or how they grow up. It's not like we ask to be born in a certain place or at a certain time. I realize that skin doesn't get any whiter than mine, and I was lucky to come from a privileged background. It sickens me to even say that something like my background is lucky, because what I am truly lucky for is that I have always had the ability to see people for people. When you meet a new person, don't think, *Oh, this is a black person or a white person or a Hispanic person or an Asian person.* Instead, think, *This is a person. I wonder what I have in common with them.* If you approach any interaction from that point of view and treat people as individuals, then you will probably be surprised at how easy it is to find common ground with every single person you meet.

One of the lowest points in my career, and a time when my mouth got me in trouble in a real way, was when I was on *The View* and something I said got misconstrued.

I was very comfortable around the other women on *The View*. Raven-Symoné is one of my best friends, I've known Whoopi for years, and Rosie has been a good friend to me for a long time. I was very used to having frank, real conversations with them about race. This particular time, we were in the midst of discussing then presidential candidate Donald Trump's appalling views on immigration. This was right after he'd called undocumented Mexican immigrants rapists and murderers, and in trying to defend the Latino community, my first mistake was to do what I always do, and fall back on sarcastic humor. I began: "If you take all the Mexican people out of America, then who is going to clean your toilet . . ." Before I could finish the comment, Rosie was instantly and rightfully offended. As the only Latina on the panel, it is her right and responsibility to defend her community. She reacted badly to the comment, as she should, but she also realized that in the heat of the moment—brought on partially by the severity of the topic and partially because of the way *The View* segments are meant to be conversational and rapid-fire (otherwise, no one would get a word in edgewise) I didn't mean what I had said in the way that it came out.

By that time, the racist ship had already sailed and I alone was to blame for that. I don't blame people for how they reacted to me, because I know what I meant and what I wanted to say, but all they heard was a sliver of my intentions that, taken out of context, was completely and utterly offensive.

This incident resulted in an outcry of people calling me racist, and I don't think that I have ever felt worse. It hurt my soul to the core of my being more than words can describe. Call me fat, call me ugly, call me a bitch and I could truly not give a fuck, but a racist is the furthest thing from who I actually am. The sensationalizing of my comment not only hurt me but hurt an entire community of people. To be misunderstood in this way hurt so much, mostly because in reality, a lot of my friends are Latino and in fact, the reason we became friends is because their households and the traditions therein are more similar to mine than any of the white friends I grew up hanging out with in America. It's been a year since that appearance on *The View*, and I still find myself apologizing.

In the end, I learned an important lesson about exercising more caution on live TV. More important, the silver lining is that my offensive comment sparked conversation and educated people on the hardships of immigrant life in the United States.

Britain may have invented colonialism, but America invented racism, and it's still shocking to me that a country that was built by immigrants is now so intent on keeping them out. I know firsthand that the joy you experience when you get your green card is almost indescribable. I cried when I got mine, because it's a symbol of acceptance and belonging. You finally know you can work, and that you no longer have to worry about being taken away from your family. It is a beautiful, beautiful thing, and America should be honored, not scared, that so many people want to move here and build their lives. Immigration is the true American dream, and now it's being turned into an American nightmare.

I grew up in a country with a lot of Muslims, and one of my best friends, Omar, is Muslim. We met at a time in our lives when we were both starving for knowledge and ready to suck up as much of it as we could. Omar taught me a lot about the customs and culture of Islam, and now I get so angry about the way people talk about Muslims.

While ISIS is busy chopping people's heads off, the rest of the Muslim community around the world is spreading peace and harmony.

I'm grateful that I was exposed to so many different cultures and types of people when I was growing up and throughout the different stages of my life. I was taught that ethnicity, religion, and sexuality were all beautiful things. It's 2017—racism doesn't have a place in our society anymore. Prejudiced beliefs don't serve a purpose and only hold people back. If you're racist, then I actually feel sorry for you, because your worldview is warped in a way that will always cut you off from new people, new cultures, and new experiences. If you judge someone by the color of their skin—or by any other facet that they have no control over—then you're not hurting them, you're only hurting yourself.

If you're not a racist, good for you, but that's not enough. You still have to stand up against discrimination. That means calling out people who make stupid comments (or idiots like me who make them accidentally) even when it doesn't affect you personally.

One time I was on a flight when one of the attendants came up to me right as I was settling in. "Before I get too crazy busy," he said, "I want to say that what you did and why you left *Fashion Police* says so much about you, and I'm so proud of the person you are, because not many people would do that." (For those of you who don't know what he is referring to, I'll first say that enough chaos has already been stirred up and more than sufficiently publicized about this incident. The important thing to note is that he was referring to a time that I didn't put my foot in my mouth and stood up for my beliefs against what I had perceived as a racist comment.)

Deep down, I always knew what that situation was about—not me fighting with a particular person but me standing up for what I believed in—but I often felt as though that got lost in the media spin. Speaking to this flight attendant let me know that people were paying attention, and I knew that even if this man was the only person in the whole world who felt like that, it was still worth all the shit I had to put up with.

I pray every day that the next generation and those to come will never know from racism. I truly believe that discrimination is fading in our generation, however slowly, and this makes me optimistic. Still, it doesn't hurt to hurry it along. And maybe even kick it in the ass on its way out the door.

*Love,*
*Kelly O*

# 23 *

............................................................................................................

# DEAR SOCIAL MEDIA

It is somewhat strange that I am writing you a letter, when I actually find you to be really boring. Don't be totally offended: To be honest, I feel like that about the whole digital world. I am part of the last generation that will ever remember what it was like not to have the Internet, and as a result, I will always be a bit nostalgic for the analog world (after all, I learned what fellatio was by looking it up in the encyclopedia). I prefer the kind of creativity that comes from hands, not from fingertips.

When I was growing up, all my photos were printed. We'd snap a picture, and then not see it for weeks or months, usually not until we were in one place long enough for me to get my film developed.

The only people who ever saw these photos were the people I decided to share them with, my friends and family. If there was a photo I hated, I did not have to show it to anyone. If something was really bad, I just tore it up, threw it in the bin, and no one ever knew it existed. None of this bullshit of pulling something out of the trash or finding it again after it's been supposedly "destroyed." I still have boxes and boxes of photographs in my apartment, and while I always have a laugh whenever I take them out to look through them, I'm very protective of them, because they represent the only private life I've got.

With digital, that privilege is gone, and this terrifies me.

Send a sexy selfie via text? It can go viral. Post something on social media, and even if you decide to delete it three seconds later, someone could already have taken a screen grab. We live in a world where once you put something out there, it's out there! There's no going back, and if that sounds ominous, it's because it is! I don't use Snapchat, because I don't really believe it disappears—when I post something, once it's up, it's up. Even if it's something that will put me in a world of pain—like tweeting at Lady Gaga to eat my shit—I own it rather than try to pretend it didn't happen and issue some fake-ass apology.

Social media is like picking your nose in the car and eating it: You think you're all alone and no one's watching, but everyone can see you! All those nasty comments you left on the page of someone you don't even know? They can be traced back to you. People like to pretend that online life and real life are two separate things. Maybe that was true back when the Internet was brand-new, but now they're one and the same. Anything you post online can be found with just a few clicks by someone who knows what they're doing.

That's why it blows my mind that people are so ruthless with celebrities—putting aside the fact that, contrary to popular belief, famous people are real people with real feelings, the vile shit you spew online can easily be traced back to you. You're not hiding.

What's more, it doesn't make the celebrity look bad, it makes you look bad. On any given week, I'll have random strangers tell me to fuck myself, kill myself, lose some weight, gain some weight, and that I'm a whore. Nine times out of ten, I don't pay attention to these kinds of comments and don't click on the profiles to see who wrote them. Every once in a while, though, something will hit in just the right place, and I get sad about it. The comments don't affect me personally—at this point in my life, being called fat doesn't have much of an effect—but I'm sad for the person who wrote it and for humanity in general. I once got a series of particularly nasty comments telling me I should just go kill myself. When I finally clicked through to see the person writing them—which I never do unless I think someone might actually be dangerous and wish me real harm—the cunt's Instagram bio read "Proud mother and grandmother" and listed all the charities she worked with!

If you're writing horrible, hateful things to someone you don't even know, something must be wrong in your life. There is no way you are happy, healthy, or fulfilled. If you were, you wouldn't have time to do these kinds of things, and what's more—you wouldn't want to!

Social media teaches us that we must judge or be judged, so it's no wonder that young women feel so much pressure to be perfect and that their value lies in their looks. When I posted about amfAR after attending their generationCURE benefit, I was shocked to see that the message about HIV/AIDS research had been overshadowed by commenters talking about . . . my hair.

I'll often get people telling me to lose weight and gain weight in the comments on the same photo. "I liked her better when she was skinny," someone will comment, while someone else writes, "Fat Kelly is my fav." It all makes me want to bang my head (and my haircut that apparently no one likes) against the wall, but instead I just sign off.

I screwed up a lot in the early days of social media, because I was still trying to understand it and figure it out. Since then, there have been other moments—not lapses or fuck-ups, but intentional moments—in which my need to protect either myself or my family have trumped my need to obey my own social media etiquette. In these moments, I try not to judge myself because I am human and no matter what I believe, I will always—*always*—follow my instinct to first and foremost protect my family.

On a page or screen, words are just in black and white. They can be easily misinterpreted, and this creates so much aggression and anger. I have said things I shouldn't have, and too often I responded to comments, thinking I could squash the negativity when in reality I was giving people what they wanted—attention—and throwing more fuel on a fire that did not deserve my time in the first place.

I used to spend a lot of time trying to figure out what it was that people wanted to see on my social media, and the only conclusion that I came to was that I have no clue. You can't make everyone happy, nor can you predict what people like, because everyone has a different opinion and different tastes. What I think will get the most likes often turns out to be stuff no one else cares about, and vice versa.

The only thing I can do is be true to myself and think about what I post before I post it. I try to represent myself as honestly as possible, while most people put a lot of time and effort into constructing their social media presence to be the person they wish they were. We all live in a filtered world—not just in Hollywood but everywhere. People spend a lot of time editing and filtering their lives on social media so they always look good. Is that really you on your Instagram, or is that the person you wish you were? If you only ever acknowledge your best side, eventually you're going to be half a person.

My Instagram consists mostly of pictures of me in gym clothes, or doing something stupid (like getting locked in my own bathroom). You will just as easily see me on a red carpet as you will in the back garden, snail hunting with my niece. I never made a conscious decision to do this; it just happened because those are the moments that make me different and make me who I am. And of course, I may put a filter on a photo here and there, but I'm not into manipulating my face, since everyone knows what I fucking look like. Other than my vagina, there's not a lot of me that the world hasn't seen, so trying to pretend to be something I'm not would be a big waste of time.

When people start talking about social media—who liked their post on Instagram, who said what on Twitter—I zone out. I might as well be a *Peanuts* character listening to a grown-up talk: "*Wawawawah, wawawawah, wawawawah.*" It is just noise and I do not care, but it scares me how much other people do. I do not think that is normal. It is not something worth wasting your emotions on. If you are looking for something to be angry about, put your phone down and look up. There are plenty of things in this world into which you can channel your anger to turn it into something positive.

 *Love,*
*Kelly O*

# 24 *

........................................................................................

# DEAR SEAT SPRINKLERS

You. Know. Who. You. Are.

You breeze out of the stall with your not-a-hair-out-of-place Brazilian blowout, your gigantic Canal Street Birkin bag, and your brows that were done by Anastasia herself, looking like the picture-perfect perception of class and good grooming. You glide over to the mirror to check your lip gloss and toss a slightly cunty smirk at those of us still waiting in line to use the loo. Meanwhile, you leave knowing full well that your secretly disgusting self has just pissed all over the fucking seat!

We've all been there—that moment when you unsuspectingly walk into a women's bathroom in a nice, upscale establishment to find that the toilet seat looks like it has just been left out in acid rain. If I had a dollar for every time I've wiped pee off a seat in a public toilet, I could just hire my own port-a-loo to follow me wherever I went so I'd never have to deal with it again.

Why, you might ask, do I bother to clean up after you? Why don't I just hover and spray like everyone else? It's simple—because I don't want anyone going in after me and coming out thinking, *That Kelly Osbourne is a filthy pisser!*

Women's toilets will always confuse me. In some ways, they're estrogen dumping sites that are guided by strict rules of courtesy and conduct. We know not to giggle when the girl in the stall at the end fuffs,** and we'll gladly offer up our last tampon to a stranger in distress to save her from date-night disaster. Enter a public women's restroom crying because someone has just been mean to you, and you will more than likely make at least three new best friends for the night who vow to spill their drinks on the asshole when they walk by his table.

**\*\* TRANSLATION**

Fuffs

My slang for when a girl farts as she's hovering over the toilet

Yet for some reason, once we're actually in the stall, it's *Mad Max*, every woman for herself.

There are those who don't flush, as if they're so anxious to get out and look at themselves in the mirror that they can't be bothered to spend the extra two-point-five seconds it takes to make sure everything they've left behind has been flushed away. Or those who can't be fucked to find a trash can when they're surfing the crimson wave and think the best place for their bloody massacre of vaginal mess is floating in the toilet or thrown in a corner. And the girls who breeze straight on out without bothering to even pretend to wash their hands: If I see you do that, I will judge, and judge harshly! Also, get out of my way, because I certainly don't want to touch anything you've touched.

I've now taken to using the men's facilities whenever they're available, because I usually find them to be cleaner. That is certainly saying something, because in case you somehow missed it, I grew up on a tour bus!

So why does this piss me off so much? One, because it's gross, and I've seen some horrible things that I can never unsee. Two, I believe in manners. I know, go ahead and call me old-fashioned. We live in an age of senseless evil, so common courtesy definitely seems as out-of-date as a Motorola pager, but I still believe that we should treat other people as we want to be treated. That means not assuming we're so important that we don't have to respect shared space. Do you want to clean up after someone else? Certainly not. So why would you expect someone else to clean up after you? If you're one of those delicate flowers who can't imagine the back of her thighs touching the cold, hard porcelain throne, then by all means, hover away. Just take a half second to wipe down the seat, flush, and then immediately wash your hands. It's that easy.

Though I do understand that sometimes we find ourselves in a place where the toilets simply aren't an option—either because they don't exist, or because you're at someplace like an outdoor music festival, where all the people on drugs have turned the toilets into plastic buckets of hot shit that have been baking in the sun all day. No one fucks up a bathroom like a druggie, which is somewhat ironic, since you would think that with as much time as they spend in there, they especially would have a vested interest in keeping things clean.

This reminds me of when I got in trouble at the Groucho Club in London for waging my own private war against cokeheads and their abuse of the toilets. This is the thing about coke—people like to pretend it's glamorous, but really, it's just powder most likely made with everything under the standard kitchen sink, including rat poison, that people are snorting up their noses off the back of the shitter. So there I was at the Groucho with a mean British pop star (who will remain unnamed) and all of her mean, twatty friends. They were high and acting as though they were the first people to have ever discovered cocaine. Dinner grew cold as they made trip after trip after trip to the loo, coming back to ignore their food and waffle on about nothing with white shit caked in the corners of their mouth.

I was bored out of my skull and feeling a bit mischievous, when inspiration struck. I took Vaseline (which every girl should have in her bag) and smeared it across every flat surface on and around the toilet. (I just want to take a minute to point out that at a lot of public places in Britain don't have tanks on the back of the toilet, so, I shit you not—pun intended—people sniff coke off the very same seat they refused to sit their ass on!) Then I stood outside the loo and waited for each patron to go back in. Vaseline absorbs cocaine, and sure enough, within minutes I heard screaming. "Aw, fuck! Shit! Fuck!" I laughed my ass off. Of course, it was pretty obvious to everyone who was responsible for turning their expensive bags of devil's dandruff into worthless mounds of goo. I was severely reprimanded by management, but was it worth it? Absolutely.

I digress. What I am saying is that sometimes you will find yourself in a place where even wiping down the seat can't save you. These are drastic circumstances, by all means, so I'm going to share with you a strategy I've learned from a life lived at concerts.

Rule number one: Always wear a long, flowy skirt. It's comfortable for sitting cross-legged on the ground, but it will also save you from having to use the same toilet as a hundred thousand other people. Avoid wearing anything with buttons or complicated straps, and God forbid, if you make the mistake of wearing a romper, you will find yourself in a circle of hell.

Rule number two: Wear a thong. You'll learn why in a minute.

Rule number three: Chances are you've got this already, but make sure to carry a giant purse or backpack to hold all your stuff.

Now that you're dressed appropriately and have everything you need, when it comes time for a wee and you can't hold it any longer, find an out-of-the-way spot where there's grass. Drop your giant bag or backpack on the ground and squat down next to it while acting like you are digging for something in your bag—knees out and the skirt covering everything. Then move the thong to one side, start to paw through your purse, and let it flow. If anyone looks at you, it's like, "Do-do-do, just squatting here to dig through my bag and trying to find my lipstick . . . Definitely not peeing on the grass right here, oh no, not me."

If you have a friend with you, this is your wingman. Make conversation and don't break eye contact. No one has the balls to take a piss on the floor of a public place while having a conversation with someone, right? Then when you're finished, just stand, use some anti-bac gel to clean your hands, and walk off. No one will ever know.

Oh, and here's another tip: You might want to watch where you sit . . .

 *Love,*
*Kelly O*

# 25*

# DEAR GROWING UP

Here we are . . .

This past Christmas, there was this whole big argument in my house—just like every Christmas—when Dad turned to me and said, "You're not a baby anymore, you're not a fucking child!" My behavior hadn't warranted that response in any way. Where did this "child" shit come from? What did I do?

A few days later, it hit me: It was because my parents want me to still be their little Kelly Tots. Except for when it's convenient for them, of course. Then I am an adult. This is probably a big part of why I get so lost mentally in the role I play in my family versus the role I play in my own life, and have such a hard time thinking of myself as either an adult or a child. I don't always feel like a "grown-up," but I don't always feel like a kid, either.

I remember when I started to having a strange feeling, and I had no idea what it was. It was there in the morning when I'd wake up at four A.M. for work, and I'd notice it at night, when I was getting stuff out of the refrigerator to make for dinner. It would creep up and give me a little reminder tap on the shoulder, then disappear just as quickly.

The feeling said something had changed. Something was different from what it had ever been before. I kept wondering, *What is this feeling? What is it?* Then it finally hit me one day when I was filling out a form. I had gotten to the part where I had to enter my age, and I had to tick a whole new box. As soon as I did, I immediately knew what that feeling was: I felt old.

After years of trying to avoid and escape it, adulthood had gone and fucking crept up on me!

For a long time, after a childhood of being exposed to all kinds of adult behaviors and situations (including dealing with the thought of losing Mum when she had cancer), and even after I was living on my own, working, and paying all my own bills, people still primarily saw me as Sharon and Ozzy's little girl, which made it hard for me to convince people—especially myself—that I am an adult. When I was twenty-nine, I made the *Forbes* 30 Under 30 list, and a life-altering emotional shift took place. It was the biggest fuck-you to anyone who had ever doubted my maturity, hard work, and career.

I was on a flight to London. As soon as we touched down, I turned my phone on to check work e-mails only to see an e-mail with the subject line "CONGRATULATIONS." I did not even know my name had been submitted, and I immediately burst into the happiest of happy tears, because no parent can get you on that list. This meant people were recognizing me for me and what I had accomplished outside my family. The feeling of pride was one of the most amazing I have ever experienced.

Turning thirty doesn't mean what it used to. It used to mean you were entering the second stage of your adult life—most likely having a kid or two, a husband, and knowing some shit about wine from various trips to Napa.

What does thirty mean today? Most thirty-year-olds I know now have not done any of those things. A lot of them don't even have jobs and are still living with their parents.

I celebrated my thirtieth birthday with a party at the Houdini mansion. It is the house that the famous magician Harry Houdini lived in and it is filled with secrets, like a trap door that leads to an underground tunnel that takes you to the estate across the street, where Houdini supposedly kept his lover a secret from his wife.

The theme of the party was *Rocky Horror Picture Show*, which was my favorite movie as a little kid and remains so to this day. Some little girls grow up watching *Annie* and singing, "Tomorrow, tomorrow, I love you, tomorrow . . ." whereas I grew up knowing the words to "Sweet Transvestite" and "Touch Me." I thought "I wanna be dirty" actually meant in-the-mud dirt, and that someone needed to wash his hands and take a bath.

All the party guests came dressed for the theme. My hairstylist Ryan came as Riff Raff, my friend Chris was Dr. Frank-N-Furter. I dressed as Magenta for the first half, then midway through traded the French maid look for Columbia's mouse ears and pajamas. It wasn't one of those parties where everyone gets shitty and passes out, like most do when they turn twenty-one, but we did stay up all night, went for a morning hike (me still in Columbia's pajamas), and swam in the pool. It was one of the best nights of my life.

The self-indulgent adolescent inside each of us creates a delusion that being a grown-up is supposed to always be boring, and let's not forget, filled with the R-word: responsibility. I have been many things, but boring has never and will never be one of them. I think adulthood comes in many colors, including lavender. (Are you reading this, Mum?) While some of those things I'd always associated with being an adult, like getting married or becoming a parent, might signify that someone has grown up, it no more makes any of us a grown-up than a leather jacket makes someone a rebel.

The process of growing up is actually a more complicated thing than anyone gives it credit for. If it were easy, then more people would do it and not end up stuck in a vicious Peter Pan cycle. To truly grow up, you have to change the way you think, and you have to take risks. In no way am I saying you have to change who you are, but you absolutely have to take the big R-word for your actions. You have to stop blaming everyone else for your circumstances, and instead look at where you are in *your* life and what your part in it is. Then, you can figure out what you did to get where you are and where to go from there. Never forget, until the day you have children, your life belongs to you and you alone.

A perfect example of this is my father. One of his first jobs was testing car horns at a factory. His job consisted of him honking a car horn every three seconds inside a room with one other person. On his first day at work, he looked at the man next to him and noticed his gold watch. Over the blaring sound of car horns, he tried to tell this man how much he liked his watch.

"I really like your watch."

"WHAT?!"

"I really like your watch."

"You WHAT?!"

"Your watch. I really like it." He gestured to his wrist.

The guy yelled, louder than the car horns, "Oh, thanks, mate. I got it from the company for working here thirty years."

Very quickly my dad realized that not only was this guy deaf, but it would take thirty years to have something that he loved, like this watch that the guy hadn't even paid for himself. He decided then and there to say, "Fuck this, I'm out."

His mum was pissed because he'd given up what many people considered a very good job, but then a few days later, Tony Iommi and Geezer Butler came knocking on Dad's door, and we all know what happened next: the invention of heavy metal.

Knowing what you don't want to do with your life is a step toward knowing what you *do* want to do, and if Dad hadn't had the courage to take that risk, then I wouldn't be here and you'd be reading some other book. The world is always changing, and if you can't change with it, you're going to get left behind.

A lot of the friends I have now are people I've known since I was a teenager. Some friends and I always say we've known one another for ten years, even though now it's more like fifteen, and I can see a big difference between the ones who changed and the ones who didn't. The ones who changed are successful, and the ones who haven't are struggling, still doing the same thing they were a decade ago. I think we all have these friends—they're the ones who look like they've aged twenty years, even though it's only been two years since you last saw them.

When I lived in London, a lot of my friends were in bands or hosted club nights. We went out *all* the time, because we were twenty-one and staying in seemed a fate worse than death. Now most of us laugh about those nights, but I know a few people who are still living them, going out and getting fucked up all the time. They aren't living month to month, but day to day. Some of them have kids, and the parents are coming home from a night out when the kids are waking up. "Mummy, why do you have on the same clothes you had on yesterday? Did you sleep in them?"

Happiness is success. You can be poor as fuck or rich as fuck, but if you're not happy with who you are, then you're not successful. That's why you see celebrities, people who seem to have everything, who still hate themselves. Wealthy people tend to moan on and on about how successful they are, but would they need to brag if they were truly happy? Probably not.

You become an adult when you stop wanting all the things you once thought would make you happy (a bunch of money, a closetful of shoes, a fit** boyfriend), and instead just want to be the best *you* that you can be, not just for yourself, but for the greater good.

I notice these changes in myself in little ways. When a bunch of friends came to Los Angeles from the UK for an awards show, one of them asked me, "Do you know where we can get some gear?"** Even though I used to be so accustomed to that question, hearing it now, I was almost shocked. "Oh," I said, and then thought long and hard. I knew a friend of a friend with a med card who could maybe get them some weed, but other than that, I had no idea who to call.

Drug dealers were not a part of my life anymore, and that was a great feeling.

I've completely Benjamin Buttoned on my morals, and in some ways, I think I'm more innocent than I've ever been. A while back, I was driving with my niece Pearl when a Katy Perry song came on the radio. I love Katy and have known her since she was Kate Hudson, and love her music and think she's had an amazing career, but as I sang along, "You can put your hands on me with your . . ." I had a sudden panic attack. *I can't sing a song that alludes to sex to my four-year-old niece!* I thought and quickly switched channels. Pearl kept laughing and had no idea, but it hit me: *Oh my God, I've changed.*

I have never been a rebel in the traditional sense, because with parents like mine, what would I rebel against? No matter how old I get, there will always be a little anarchist who lives inside me. She loves to pitch a fit and scream, "No one understands me," but as I get older, I realize that's not true. We get to pick our friends, so we can stop trying to get all our validation from our family. You can stop being mad at your parents, because you now understand that they're human, too.

One of the major perks of being a grown-up is that (some workplaces aside) you really don't have to be around people who don't get you. Age isn't a factor in who I choose to be around, but maturity is. I've been very close with people who are much older than I am, like Joan, or younger, like Ava, Kelly Cutrone's teenage daughter.

Denying your age is the official hobby of Hollywood, but I'm bloody embracing mine. There were times in my life when I never expected that I'd make it to thirty, much less enjoy it when I got there.

It's just going to get better from here. Forty? Bring it on. Being an old lady? I can't wait—my inner eighty-year-old is already clawing out with her acrylics. I plan on getting as much Botox as womanly possible (Joan taught me well), always having purple hair, and giving even fewer fucks than I do now.

*Love,*
*Kelly O*

# ACKNOWLEDGMENTS

Thank you to my family: Mum, Dad, Jack, Aimee, Lisa, Pearl, Andy Rose, Louis, Louise, Mia, Elija, and Saba Teklehaymanot. Thank you for being my guardian angels.

Fleur Newman and Sammy Barratt-Singh: Together we truly are the three best friends that anyone could have. You are my true sisters!

Thanks to extraordinary friends: Colin and Metta Newman, Sue and Graham Hall, Joan Rivers, Melissa Rivers, Cooper Rivers, Ethan Sugar, Mike Einziger, José Pasillas, Simone Francese, Richard Kavanagh, Jeannie Mai, Maxine Gittens, Oz, Louie Vito, Simon Huck, Kim Kardashian, Nicole Richie, Melissa Rosenfield, Robert Ramsey, Christian Siriano, Aya T. Kanai, Hannah Jeter, Tim Gunn, Mike Flom, Vicky Vox, Jeff Beacher, Blake Wood, Braydon Szafranski, Catriona, Sshh Starkey, Raven-Symoné, Zendaya, Sophie Monk, Dom DeLuca, Jody Oli, Fernando Barraza, Whitney Plowman, Zac Posen, Betsey Johnson, Dita Von Teese, Richard K, and George Kotsiopoulos.

Omar Kahn: The day we found each other was fate. In fact, it was magic because that is what you are—magic. I love you so much.

Kelly and Ava Cutrone (aka Ava Bieber): To say we are close friends is not enough. We are family for life. Without the love, support, and guidance you so selflessly give to me, I not only would never have finished this book but I would be utterly lost without you both. I was a wounded bird that you taught to fly again. Ava, not a day goes by that I don't learn something new from you and love your sassy ass more and more. I am your big sister. I will always be here for you, no matter what. Kelly, my Mumma Witch, my Scorpio sister, my roommate, my partner in crime, we have come so far from the day our birthday cakes got switched. I got a cake with a pair of tits on it, and you got a cake wishing you a happy twenty-first birthday. From there, our beautiful journey began, and it's one that I know will never end.

Denika Bedrossian: There is no one in this world who makes me feel beautiful the way you do. Not just because of the way you do my makeup but the true friendship that you provide daily. You make the toughest days a breeze, made me an honorary member of your Armenian family, and never fail to put me in check. You are one hell of a badass witch who always tells it like it is.

Luke Trembath (Dingo): From the day we both moved to this foreign land that we call Hollyweird, we have been inseparable. When my brother did not want to hang out with me anymore because I was an annoying dork, you picked up where he left off. Thank you for being there every step of the way when most people would have jumped ship. We may not be related by blood but I see you as my brother. You are a member of my family. (Sometimes I feel like my mother loves you more than she loves me.) PS: To any of our mutual friends who are reading this: No, Dingo and I have never hooked up. For God's sake, I have never even seen his penis and we pretty much live together. PPS: To all your ex-girlfriends who treated me like shit: Fuck you.

Rob Moore: Fuck you, too! I love you, ya dork.

Jacob Thomson: I have been there for you since the day you were born and I will be here for you until the day I die.

Michael Kozac: Aunt Tuna, thank you for making every day an

experience of a lifetime and being one of the few people in this world who truly understands my lunacy!

Louis van Amstel: One of the first things I ever said to you was, "You got the wrong partner!" I could not have been more wrong. You not only changed my life but you saved it, too. Thank you for never giving up on me and for teaching me how to look after my mind, body, and soul, and what dedication really means. I will credit you until the day I leave this world for turning me into the woman I am today. However, I will never get over the fact that you did this through fucking ballroom dancing. I love you more than you will ever understand.

Thank you to all my colleagues and contributors: Jasen Kaplan, Ryan Randel, John Stapleton, Ross Mathews, Frankie Hernandez, Joseph DiMaggio, Tom Chadwick, Michael Guarracino, John Fenton, Steven Grossman, Fergie, Brad Goreski, Kathy Griffin, Nancy Davis, Joanna Coles, Adam Lambert, Jason Bolden, Geezer and Gloria Butler, Kelly Ward, Tom Ruegger, Jesse Harnell, Steve Varga, Lucas Varga, Scarlett Varga, Mimi Varga, Chris and Poppy Abrego, Jay Mighall, Bob Troy, Jennifer Holliday, Philip Battiade, Veronica Jahanfard, Zachary Russo, and Jordan Manikin.

Melinda Varga: You went from one of my few female friends on tour to my nanny, to my assistant—until my mum stole you—to a person not just I but my whole family and in fact the entire Osbourne enterprise could not function without. Please don't ever leave us, as we would be fucked without you.

Brooke Dulien: Thank you for being my style guru. You taught me almost everything I know when it comes to fashion. You even bought me my first pair of heels. However, I will never stop wearing my sports bras.

Gary Orkin: I'm sorry that I have driven you crazy because I spend and donate too much money. I'm also sorry for contributing not only to you going gray but to making you pull your hair out. All jokes aside, thank you, Gary.

Adam Griffin, my manager: Wow . . . I bet you never realized how much you had cut out for you when we decided to work with each other! Thank you for always being the calm through the storm and getting me through this crazy journey we are on. I can't wait to climb more mountains with you!

Diandra Younesi: Thank you for always being a badass bitch.

Todd Jacobs: Thank you for believing in me when no one else did. Everything I have built in the past twelve years has been because of you. You are the best agent in the world. I have no idea how you took me from a grain of sand and turned me into a diamond, but you did. You achieved what I and most others viewed as the impossible. You are my zen master and I love you.

Evan Warner: Thank you for being not only the best TV agent in the biz but my dear friend and stagecoach partner in crime. You are like my weird uncle that I'm not sure I even wanted but am so lucky to have. I could never have finished this book without the way you stepped up. You are the best.

Justin Ongert: Thank you for putting the ass in the class of my team!

Marcel Pariseau: The day you took me on was life-changing. There is no person's opinion that I respect more than yours. Not a day goes by that I don't feel honored to work with you. I love you. In fact, I'm obsessed with you.

Joey Monroe: Thank you for being you. I know what a pain in the ass I am to work with due to my lack of inner filter, but you tackle every situation I get us into head-on because you know that I always have the best of intentions. You never vocalize any judgment (although your face does a good enough job of saying it for you). You are one of my favorite people to work with, and I can't wait for our next PJ party!

Gary Farrow: Thank you for always scaring the shit out of me with your brutal honesty. I fucking love you. However, I hate that you are always right!

Erin Malone: I can't even imagine what a nightmare I was during the three-year process of finishing this book, but you are one badass agent and I could not have done this without you.

Kerri Kolen: You truly are the real-life Carrie Bradshaw. Thank you for holding my hand through this crazy journey. From the second I met you, I knew that there was no other publisher I wanted to write this book with. I apologize in advance if Baby Quinn is born, with a mouth like a sailor. That's not a joke; I really am sorry. By the time this book is published, Baby Quinn, you will finally be born and I want to thank you for lending me your mumma. When most first-time mothers are freaking out over what to expect when they're expecting, your mumma was a fearless iron woman who never missed a Bar Method class and never ceased to amaze me when she showed up wearing the most badass outfits (including heels), carrying a bag that must have weighed ten thousand pounds. Although it may take you more than a few years to realize this, trust me when I say that your mum is one badass bitch!

Kate Williams: I will never say that I wrote this book all by myself or refer to you as my "ghostwriter." We did this together. At this point, I don't think there is a single person in this world who knows more about me—or wants to—than you do. You not only had to put up with me and the insanity that revolves around me, you did it with such grace. The first day we met, I thought to myself, *I'm going to unintentionally destroy this fragile little mouse with my big mouth!* Little did I know how wrong I was. You somehow always managed to keep me calm and make me laugh when all I wanted to do was cry. It's true what they say: It's the quiet ones you have to watch out for, because without any shadow of a doubt in my mind, you are the number one badass bitch with whom I had the honor of working on this book. You even managed to trump Kerri, which is hard to do. To say thank you is not enough, but I will say it anyway. Thank you! I fucking adore you!

Karen Gottlieb: You are one hell of a badass bitch and it is an honor to work with you.

To all the badass bitches at Putnam: Ivan Held, Christine Ball, Sally Kim, Anabel Pasarow, Alexis Welby, Ashley Hewlett, Ashley McClay, Carrie Swetonic, Emily Ollis, Meredith Dros, Melissa Solis, Janice Kurzius, Claire Vaccaro, Monica Benalcazar, and Kaitlin Kall.